Check Your Homelife

by Knofel Staton

STANDARD PUBLISHING
Cincinnati, Ohio   39973

For Consideration or Discussion at the end of each chapter was prepared by Bruce R. Parmenter.

Scripture quotations are from the New American Standard Bible, © The Lockman Foundation 1960, 1962, 1963, 1968, 1971, 1972, 1973, 1975, 1977.

Library of Congress Cataloging in Publication Data:
Staton, Knofel.
　Check your homelife.
　1. Family—Religious life. 2. Family. I. Title.
　BV4526.2.S7　　　　　1983　　　　　646.7'8　　　　　82-19600
　ISBN 0-87239-649-5

Dedication

To the five wonderful people who have taken me in when I didn't deserve to be taken in: Julia, Randy, Rena, Rhonda, and Rachel.

Appreciation

To my wife, Julia, who served as my editor and made many valuable suggestions; to the three girls who did all the typing—Beverly Flick, Linda Merold, and Linda Webb.

Contents

Sharing the thoughts of his own heart, the author may express views that are not entirely consistent with those of the publisher.

Introduction

The need of meaningful sharing (giving and taking) within the community is felt by every human. No one should live alone; indeed, no one develops well alone. God makes it clear that human development comes through interpersonal sharing in love. Yet the development of man "made in the image of God" is facing a powerful enemy called individualism, which threatens to destroy the concept of the community. One of the tragedies of this battle is that whatever threatens the individual's community also threatens the community's individual. Nowhere is this more vividly seen than in the smallest community—the home.

The separate schedules of family members keep them apart. The television set tends to make us more cloistered than communicative. The automobile pulls us away from home. When each person does "his own thing," unmet needs of the individuals emerge, instead of heightening our individual maturity. Some run away from home to live in a commune where interpersonal sharing can take place. Others experiment with the drug culture or the occult culture, trying to discover or extend their selfhood through a kind of "mental community." Small sharing groups are becoming a popular experience for many.

Since the truth that people need people is becoming once more evident, it is not surprising to find a renewed interest in the family. Contemporary literature reflects a high interest in the family, even though contemporary life reveals a limited involvement in satisfying family living. The rise in the divorce rate, along with the high sale of books about family living, indicates an interest in how to succeed in family life. The tragedy is that many who are not divorced do not feel they have succeeded. They are married, but not happy.

Is there an infallible guide to successful family living? It depends on how we measure "success." If success is measured by our own wishes, the answer is no. The success of anything cannot have desire as the criterion for evaluation. The success of anything is measured by whether or not it is functioning according to its design. I might wish that my car could fly, but I can't say it is a flop if it doesn't. I must consider the car's designed purpose, and I must also determine whether or not I have treated it according to that design. It is the same when evaluating success within a family.

We must begin our search for successful family life by consulting our "God-*ufactured*" guide, the Bible. In this guide, we find both the purpose for the family, and the designed roles of individuals within the family. Live by Bible-based principles, and a happy family will result. No shortcut will work. Gimmicks must give way to God. Strategies of men must give way to the Spirit of God. Selfishness must give way to sacrifice. Then we will be on the road to becoming the kind of people God intended. We will be people created in His image and living lives worth sharing and developing, lives that foster "common oneness" in the home.

Let us consider God's design for the family. But let us do it with the willingness to change whatever needs changing. Being happy in the home depends greatly upon what kind of person each member is becoming, for this affects what kind of persons the other family members can become.

Knofel Staton
Pacific Christian College
Fullerton, California

Bending
With the Winds

1

On the eve of his ninetieth birthday, Will Durant, the world-renown philosopher-historian, shared in an interview what he called his greatest concern: "The family has gone to pieces and marriage has gone, too. This is unfortunate, because they are two forms of order that can be pillars of strength in the flux of modern life." In that interview, Durant made a statement that should cause everyone to sit up and take notice. He said, "If you get rid of the state, the family can maintain order. But get rid of the family, and you have nothing."

I would like to put Durant's last statement into the Christian context. "If you get rid of the institutional church (and it's illegal in some places to have one), the Christian family can still maintain the Christian system. But if you get rid of the Christian family, the gathering together of an institutional church would not be Christian."

It is possible to get rid of the Christian family in any culture if the Christian value system, ethics, and priorities are gradually eliminated from the family. It can happen very slowly over the span of several decades by simply bending with the current winds that blow against God's will being done in the family.

It is very important to know what kinds of trends make up our present history. Then we should ask, "How are these trends affecting me and my family?" We read about history five hundred years ago and ask, "Why couldn't those people see those trends?" In the year 2500, people will read about our present history and ask, "Why couldn't those people see those trends?" But it is not easy to spot trends when they are a part of *our* history. We are too close to it all to notice the slow movements that take place. It is important, however, that we try.

On October 27, 1975, the front cover of *U.S. News and World Report* had these words, "The American Family—Can It Survive Today's Shocks?" Here are some of the trends spotlighted:

1. Divorce rates are increasing. The divorce rate in the United States is the highest in the world. The number will double in the next fifteen years.
2. More wives run away from home than husbands.
3. Increasingly children are under the care of a single parent.
4. Nearly forty percent of wives with preschool children work outside the home.
5. Child psychiatrists are growing in demand.
6. More than thirty percent of school-age children live with parents who have been divorced at least once.
7. Over six million preschool children have working mothers, yet day-care centers are taking care of only one million of them. Many of the others are "latchkey" children who unlock an empty house and wait hours for someone to arrive.
8. Over one million children run away from home every year.
9. Suicide is the second cause of deaths among teenagers.
10. One out of ten females is a mother by the time she reaches the age of seventeen.
11. One out of nine youths is in juvenile court by the time he is eighteen.

While the above are results, following are some of the shocks hitting the American family that can alter our direction unless we allow God to stay in control.

The Shock of High Mobility

How many people do you know who have moved from one house to another during the past five years? (I've asked that question of hundreds of audiences and at least eighty percent of the hands go up.)

It's a lot different than when I was a boy growing up. I was born in our house in Illinois, in 1934. My folks got a bargain that night—two of us for $25.00. Those were the days when doctors came to the house for any reason. (I rather suspect many of us survived not because the medicine was that good, but because our doctor was also our friend. There is a lot of healing power in friendship.)

In 1939, our family of six moved into a four-room house in Fairfield, Illinois. My mother, who is in her eighties, still lives in that same house. From the time I was born, until I left for military service,

I lived in only two houses. By the time our son was twelve years old, he had already lived in eight different houses. He could remember only two of them. He lives in a highly mobile society.

High mobility does not need to destroy our families. But picking up roots often does require a lot of positive interpersonal relationships between family members.

There are several positive results of mobility: expanded experiences, new friendships, new starts with clean slates, breaking out of stereotypes, growth beyond provincialism, etc.

Moving often can have some negative effects: separation from friends, being away from family support groups—aunts, uncles, parents, grandparents, etc., feelings of insecurity, feelings of not belonging to a community, lack of commitment to the community, thus, fewer people taking functional interest in such things as schools, elections, city council meetings, etc., higher rates of vandalism in the community. Transplanting roots can be counter productive to growth for some. Teenagers are especially vulnerable when taken away from their close friends. Consequently, any move calls for family members to initiate special effort and time at reinforcing interpersonal relationships within the family unit in a positive manner.

Families who have to move can make that move more of a positive experience by doing the following:

1. Discuss the potential move with the whole family.
2. Outline the positive aspects of the move.
3. Take the whole family to the new location. Show the children schools, parks, area attractions, churches, etc. If possible, meet key personnel.
4. Allow the whole family to participate in the selection of the house and neighborhood.
5. Pray about the move in positive terms.
6. Have the whole family help plan and prepare for the actual move. For instance, a rummage sale could be an all family project.
7. Allow the children special times with their friends before the move. Have the friends at the house.
8. Organize preparations for the move so they're not hectic, last-minute times of harrassment and short tempers.
9. Call the church in the area to get the time of services. Also see if there are any special activities that your children might be able to participate in as soon as they arrive.

10. Have the movers pack some of the children's special items last so they can be taken out first—bikes, toys, etc.
11. Make the trip to the new location an enjoyable one.
12. At the new house, walk through it with the whole family and point out the special features.
13. Set up the children's rooms first.
14. If there are children in the neighborhood, let your children spend time with them as soon as possible.
15. Invite the youth minister to your house while you are still unpacking so he can get acquainted with your children. (You might even give him $20 to take your children and a couple of others out for a treat to help them get acquainted.)
16. Take the children to some kind of recreation as soon as possible—swimming, racquetball, miniature golf, etc.
17. Get the family involved in church activities the first Sunday. See where each child will attend his classes. Encourage him to participate in any special youth activities coming up.
18. Get involved in a Sunday-school class *immediately*. Go to the class socials. Have one at your house as soon as possible.
19. Spend a few days (Saturdays, Sunday afternoons, etc.) driving through the new city and the general area. Get a feel of how the streets are arranged and where places are located. Get oriented.
20. Within the first week, discover what is available that your children were involved in at the old location—piano lessons, ball teams, etc.
21. Go to the Chamber of Commerce the first week to get a calendar of events, brochures about the area, a map, etc. There is a gold mine of help from the Chamber of Commerce.

Moving can be fun, and it can stretch each member of the family to more stability and potentiality reaching, but it has to be worked at. Every family needs a larger community than itself to back it up. That larger community includes the church, the neighborhood, and the community at large.

The Shock of High Economy

Have you noticed how prices continue to climb? Some economists estimate the total cost of raising a child through college, which includes the lost wages of a mother who leaves the labor force for eighteen years, at around $550,000. What does high economy do for a family? It can do many things. Here are a few:

It can cause both husband and wife to work in order to make the ends meet. However, there is more than added income that results from both parents working. Here are some of the other aspects:

1. Relationships with the mate will change. Whether they will be positive or negative changes depend upon the couple. Seventy percent of couples where both work said in a survey that work pressures frequently or occasionally create a serious strain on their marriage. It is a rare woman who can work eight hours a day and come home to prepare dinner (while the husband reads the paper), help the children do homework and give baths (while the husband watches television), go to PTA or other children's events, run errands, go to the grocery store, pick up the clutter (while the husband moves in and out of television watching and nap taking), and then be an energetic queen of lovemaking at 11:00 p.m. when the husband wakes up ready for action. A working wife can begin resenting her husband if home responsibilities aren't shared. When both work outside the home, it is imperative for both to work inside the home also.

2. Relationships with the children change. One working mother said, "My working has enabled us to buy extra things for our kids. That used to alleviate some of my guilt feelings about not spending more time with them. But, to my horror, it is clear that the kids now prefer having the 'things' over spending time with me." A little nine-year-old girl saw it differently. She said, "I think that my mother should be able to work as long as she wants. She gets off at 11:30 A.M. so I can spend lots of time with her. And I love my mother bigger than the world." She was saying that she loved her mother more than all the things mother could bring home—even if she brought home everything in the world. That kind of response came from a little girl who had evidently been given positive personal attention by her mother.

Working away from home takes time away from the kids. However, that can be helped if parents rearrange some priorities when they get home. In a survey conducted by *Better Homes and Gardens* (February 1982), sixty-six percent of the women who worked outside the home spent their evening hours watching television. Both parents who work need to sit down together to discuss time, activities, and

13

commitments for family interaction. They should plan special family days that include surprises. Time with the children *each day* needs to be scheduled. The children's activities at school, church, etc. need to be a part of working parents' schedule. Work away from home does not have to result in child neglect. But it certainly can! Some experts are observing that each generation seems to be less nurturing and supportive from within the family. Babies and children do not get the intimate attention they need to grow up to become parents who nurture their own children as they should. We have got to slow down the trend.

3. Relationship with self changes. A woman's relationship with herself may change. It is easy for a working mother to feel guilty because of time away from the children and lowered housekeeping standards around the house. One woman said, "With a spouse, child, home, and job all demanding one hundred percent of me, my hardest decision each day is how I will delegate my time among my responsibilities. I feel hopelessly torn."

Some women working away from the home have their self-images raised. That can be good if they don't begin to think they don't need their husbands. The independence that a wife experiences working away from home can be either positive or negative. It depends upon how she channels it and how she uses it.

When both husband and wife work outside the home, the man's relationship with himself may change also. One study noted that many men are threatened when the wife works. The "pride" that he can provide for the family is attacked.

4. Relationships with the neighborhood can change. Being away from home can change the neighborhood to a touch-and-go area rather than an area where we participate with each other. Sometimes a working couple places too much expectation on their neighborhoods by leaving their children unattended. Some even expect the neighbors to take on more child care while both parents work.

High economy enables us to buy more than one car (although we may not be able to keep more than one going). What does that do? It can do some positive things for a family. The housewife doesn't have to sit at home waiting for the wheels to arrive before she does shopping or runs errands. It enables her to get out of the house for much-needed relief. Parents don't have to take the teenagers everywhere. They can drive themselves while the parents sit at home and worry. (Parents get their smallest amount of sleep after they've done two things—brought the baby home from the hospital and brought the car home for that same person sixteen years later.)

Multiple cars can have some negative effects (although I wouldn't want to go back to one car). A plaque in an airport gift shop read, "The family that stays together—probably has one car." There's more truth to that than at first meets the eye. I can get into one car and my wife can get into the other. We can head two different directions and do two different things—apart from each other. If we aren't careful, we can catch ourselves never doing things together. As I was growing up, when the car left, the whole family left in it. Our entire family of six always went to church in the same car for we had only one.

Not long ago I was visiting a friend who had four cars—one for each member in the family. On Sunday morning guess how many cars pulled out of that driveway for the same church parking lot? You're right—all four!

One researcher suggests that our increased mobility, enhanced by the availability of autos, has contributed significantly to the rise of immorality. Our wheels help us feel independent. We get away from the people who know us to do our own thing.

High economy, plus the availability of wheels, can help turn us into "go-aholics." We are consistently on the go. Isn't it interesting that right after we are married we can't find enough money; when money starts coming in, we can't find enough time; when we finally have enough money and time (the kids are raised), we are out of energy? It's hard to find a night to be at home with the whole family. When such a night does happen to appear on the calendar, we aren't quite sure how to handle it.

Ever feel like a stranger at home? When I was growing up, I knew where my folks were every night—at home. And that's where I was. We did things together. When six people live in a four-room house *whatever* you do you do *together*, whether you like it or not. Families today should govern and protect some family times. Here are some ideas: (1) A weekly family night, such as a Monday night. Nothing is allowed to be scheduled on top of it. This is a night for being together without television. Table games, trips, recreation, and family projects can fill the night. (2) A daily time to touch bases—perhaps a few moments after dinner. (3) A surprise "family

15

day." Occasionally we tell the kids in the morning, "Today is 'Staton Day.' " They know what that means. It means something special with the family—a trip, a special movie and snack out, the beach, seeing special sights, etc. While high economy offers us many positive benefits, it can help fragment us if we aren't careful. When Dr. Robert B. Taylor, a specialist in family medicine, was asked what is behind the sharp rise in divorce, he replied, "The biggest problem seems to be that modern society is pulling partners in different directions. Job and social pressures often demand that the married couple work apart all day and be involved in different social activities at night, giving them very little time together. Time together is very important in bonding a relationship" (Copyrighted interview in *U.S. News & World Report,* January 22, 1979).

The Shock of Television

Television is another shock that hurts the family. I am not one who says, "Throw it out." Children will not learn discernment that way. There are some programs (not many) that are good. I'm glad my children have zeen exposed to them.

Being so hooked on television that it is the automatic "activity" for the evening is devastating. Before the average child is five-years-old, he will have spent more time watching television than a college student spends in the classroom for four years study. By the time he is eighteen, he will have logged 22,000 hours watching television, 12,000 hours in school, and 700 hours in religious instruction. Guess what is influencing him most. Some sociologists are saying that the number one influence on the mind-set of children is no longer the parents, school, church, or peer groups—but television. The mind is a computer that records and retains in some dimension all the input.

Just what is going into minds hour after hour? Three television networks were surveyed recently. In one week on prime time there were 113 stabbings, 92 shootings, 168 beatings, 9 stranglings, and 179 other specific acts of violence. Spaced at five-minute intervals were cleverly planned commercials glorifying sex appeal, physical beauty, and material possessions. (Have you noticed that they never film alcohol ads on skid row?) It is not possible to pour violence and negative, interpersonal relationships into minds for hours every day and then expect that person not to have output similar to the input.

Television is really an escapism from life. One fourteen-year-old confessed, "Television is perfect to tune out the rest of the world,

16

but I don't relate with my family much because we're all too busy watching television." In one study of four- to six-year-olds, nearly half "liked TV better than daddy." Researchers also find greater tension in families with high levels of television watching, because of the failure to build relationships with each other at home.

We have television in our house, but the parents control it—not the children. Our children do not watch programs with the violence, sexual innuendos, or the super horror movies. Consequently, none of the four is hooked on television. We have many games at our house, plus a pool table and a ping-pong table. When the house is full of kids (which it usually is), television is not the thing to do. It's so boring. Who wants to be bored all night anyway?

The Shock of Age Separation

In 1950, fifty percent of American families had a grandparent living in; last year only twenty-seven percent did. We are living in a time when we are separating older folks from younger folks at nearly every experience. Our high mobility and high economy have helped us do it. High mobility has moved many of us hundreds or thousands of miles from our extended support family—grandparents, uncles, aunts, and parents. High economy has helped us put older people into human junk piles—waiting for nothing. (Many nursing homes are top-notch, absolutely delightful, but most are not. If you doubt that, just take a tour of *all* the homes in your area.)

Cultures and subcultures that last hundreds and hundreds of years have this philosophy: "The older you get, the more important and needed you are to us." (As each year ticks by, I believe that more and more—and I want others to believe it also.) That's the philosophy of many of the Asian cultures. Even the Indian subculture in this country believes it. Who are the most respected in the Indian subculture—the young bucks? No! The older chieftains.

A culture that wants to shelve its older citizens to meaninglessness is headed to the pits. The older do not glean from the younger their creativity and energetic freshness. At the same time, the younger do not glean from the older the practical wisdom that is so necessary for continual progress. Consequently, the older see little to hope for and the younger see little to build upon.

Grandparents and grandparent-kind of people are the most influential people in any country. Children love and respect their grandparents. A person who works with prisoners told me that the only persons hard-core prisoners will really listen to are their grandparents. Later in this book we will look more closely at grandparents, with practical suggestions for being a functioning grandparent.

The Shock of Humanism

Humanism is having a heyday in our educational systems, beginning in the elementary schools. At one time our educational systems were all designed to introduce students to the world, to man, and to God. We believed that learning these three subjects came from experiences, formal education, and revelation. But we have succeeded in eliminating God as a subject we need to be introduced to, and revelation as a source of education for the world, man, and God. That leaves us with humanism. Humanism does not believe there is an absolute God with absolutes by which man should live. It leaves control to the people with the biggest threat or rewards. It leaves us open to adopt any immoral activity as OK.

Consequently, our children are exposed to values that are anti-family values. They face stuff by the sixth grade I never thought anyone would face throughout a whole lifetime. The closest I got to pornography while growing up was the women's section in the Sears, Roebuck catalog, but our kids brush up against X-rated sights and sounds almost daily. What used to be reserved just for the raunchiest restroom walls, now appears in living color on theater screens and televison tubes. Our kids are being bombarded with the idea that homosexuality is an alternate life-style. They can get the pill and condoms free just for the asking; they can get abortions as easily as a tonsillectomy.

How are families handling these kinds of shocks? Some aren't doing too well. In addition to the results listed toward the beginning of this chapter, others are:

1. Since 1972 we have murdered over twelve million unborn babies. That's three times Hitler's holocaust.
2. The number one reason children die in this country is child abuse. We are the only country in the world that murders its children at a rate higher than any other death taker.
3. Mothers are bailing out. In 1950, for every mother who ran away from home, three hundred fathers did it. Today for every father who runs away from home, two mothers do.
4. Incest is on the increase at an alarming rate. One-third of the

people involved in incest are children under six-years-old.
5. The divorce rate is approaching one divorce for every two marriages.

But that's enough negativism. Instead of negative facts, we need to spend time with positive understandings and practical suggestions. We need to spend time looking for solutions, not just analyzing problems. The place to begin is the Bible. The place to begin in the Bible is God's first teaching about a husband and a wife. We will turn to that next.

For Consideration or Discussion

1. How many times has your family moved in the last ten years?
2. How have those moves affected your family? Negatively. Positively.
3. What resources helped you in making positive adjustments to those moves?
4. Is your family experiencing greater or lesser financial difficulty than you were five years ago?
5. If the answer to the above question is "greater difficulty," what coping methods has your family used to deal with financial stress?
6. If the answer to 4 was "lesser," has the increased prosperity been reflected in increased financial giving to the church or other worthy causes? Yes_____ No_____
7. When your family was under financial stress, did you discontinue your giving to the church? Yes_____ No_____ Somewhat_____
8. How much time would you estimate your family spends watching TV each day?
9. Do you know what kind of programs your children are watching? Yes_____ No_____
10. Have you, as a parent, tried to develop activities for the family which would represent alternatives to watching TV? Yes_____ No_____

We Need
Each Other
2

We live in a society that worships independence and makes it a weakness to admit needing someone else. "Pulling your own strings" is the macho thing to do.

Ever live on or near a farm? The dependency differences between newborn animals and human babies are striking. Ever see a mother hen carry a baby chick around for a whole year? Ever see a calf roll, crawl, and months later walk?

Not only do humans need each other at birth; we need each other throughout our entire lifetime. That's why so much of Biblical teaching has to do with relationships with one another. A few years ago a popular song said, "People who need people are the luckiest people in the world."

Probably the greatest threat to a marriage is not the economy, sex, or separations, but the western philosophy of super independence. The first hurdle to clear in marriage is for husband and wife to admit that they really do need each other. And notice, it is a two-way street; none of this, "You need me, but I don't need you."

After five days of excitedly shouting, "It is good," God created man on the sixth day. When God carefully looked over what He created in that man, He declared, "It is not good." (Not so many "amens" ladies.) But God did not say that man wasn't good. After all, He was made in the image of God. What then wasn't good? "It is not good for the man to be alone" (Genesis 2:18).

What a shocking, unbelievable statement. How could that man be alone? He had all the animals as pets, and God himself to talk with and walk with.

It was God and Adam; and Adam was experiencing aloneness. That truth shatters traditional thinking. I used to think, "Give me God and me. That's all I need." But that was the first thing God said was not good. That's not because God is insufficient, but because God made man to need others. The Hebrew word for alone is a sense of helplessness and restlessness.

We are "God-*ufactured*" people and the Designer who knows us well declared, "I will make him a helper suitable for him" (Genesis 2:18). The Hebrew word for helper is normally used in the Old Testament to refer to God's help (Exodus 18:4; Deuteronomy 33:7, 26, 29; Psalm 20:2; 33:20; 89:19; 115:9-11; 121:1, 2; 124:8). Except for the usage in Genesis 2, it is used in a negative way when referring to human help (Isaiah 30:5; Ezekiel 12:14; Daniel 11:34; Hosea 13:9).

Why would a word normally used to refer to God's help be used to refer to the woman's help? That's easy to answer. God helps the male through the woman. In fact, the woman takes up the slack when man lacks. No wonder God didn't say that His creation was *very* good until after He had created both the man and the woman (Genesis 1:31). Both provided the balance needed.

The Hebrew word for "suitable" means one who corresponds with the other, one who complements the other, one who fits what is before the other. It is a beautiful word that communicates interdependence. Male and female need one another because they are different. The female has some things to offer that the male doesn't. In fact, he "picks up" many of her positive contributions. The male has some things to offer that the female doesn't. She picks up many of his positive traits.

Male and female are different in many ways. We differ biologically. If the "X" gets to the egg first, it's a girl. If the "Y" gets to the egg first, it's a boy. We start out with a different biological genetic code. A medical doctor told me not long ago that scientists discovered that every cell in a female and male have some differences. Generally, a female has a higher voice than a male, larger lungs, a faster heartbeat, and a larger stomach. Generally, a female runs differently from a male, and throws a ball differently. Generally speaking, a female can conceive children while a male can beget children. We are biologically different.

Even the male/female brains are organized differently. The male speech is controlled by only the left hemisphere of his brain. But the woman's speech covers the whole brain. (One man has observed that that means the only way to silence a woman is to destroy the whole brain. But a woman suggests that that means everything a man says is half-wit.)

There are some other differences. Generally speaking, a male has a bigger ego problem than a female. Have you noticed that we men think we know *everything* about—guess what—*everything,* and we think we are wrong about what—nothing! For instance, have you ever been with your husband when he got lost? (I know about it from myself. I have decided that if gasoline reaches $5.00 a gallon, I will still drive around forty-five minutes before I'll stop and tell someone who has never seen me before—and he'll never see me again, I'll make sure of that—"I'm lost. How do I find . . . ?")

Dr. Henry Brandt tells a classic story on himself. He and his wife were between Detroit and Chicago. Dr. Brandt had a lectureship to do in Chicago. As they made a turn to get onto the interstate for Chicago, his wife, said, "Henry, that's the wrong turn. This is the way to Detroit." He replied, "I know where I'm going." On the interstate, he saw a big green sign that said "Detroit ____ miles." He said that he thought to himself, "What will teenagers do next? Now they are changing highway signs in the middle of the night." So he kept on driving toward "Chicago." Then he saw the second green sign, "Detroit ____ miles." He thought, "I've got to try one more sign." A few more miles down the road there it was, the third green sign, "Detroit ____ miles." Brandt said, "You may not believe it, but I drove seventy miles trying to figure out 'How can I get to Chicago without turning this thing around?' " Male ego!

But women have some oddities, too. One of them is this. A woman cannot handle well being taken for granted. She needs to be noticed and talked with. She needs those tender touches, special unexpected gifts, and complimentary words. (Men need those, too, but perhaps not as often as women.) She needs to hear those three magic words often: "I love you." And, fellows, they aren't difficult words to memorize. Work on it for a week—at least. But it's not just the words; it's the tone of voice that communicates. Coming across as a grouchy bear who has just awakened suddenly with the shout, "I love you," won't work. Tone of voice accounts for thirty-eight percent of effective communication.

Male and female are made holistically. Sex refers to the whole person, not just certain parts of the body. A male is male from head to toe, and so is a female, female from head to toe. The physique of male/female is related to the total personhood. The male physique is designed to be aggressive and penetrative, and his "total" male identity matches it. Generally, men are concerned with conquering and mastering.

A man is concerned with "what works," whether it helps to build or to destroy. Consequently, he wants to get on with such things as technological triumph, even if the "triumph" threatens society.

The woman's physique is tied in with a different kind of concern. Erik Erikson, a keen authority on human development, says that the inner space of woman is designed to bear and nurture new life. Erikson observes that the woman's inner space corresponds with her total self. The woman has a predisposition to bring to relationships concerns such as preservation, nurturing, peacemaking, and survival. Generally speaking, a woman has more empathy, has more acceptance of reality, is more resistant to some man-killing diseases, is more easily touched and touchable, and recovers faster to act again. Generally, she will "take pain" to understand and alleviate suffering, and she can train others in forbearance necessary to stand unavoidable pain. She adapts easier.

The female "mothering instinct" and the male "mastering instinct" provide the necessary balance for any society. Without the mothering instinct, we would destroy each other. Without the mastering instinct, we would not make steady progress dominating, harnessing, and using our environment.

So when God said, "It is not good for the man to be alone," He had the whole society in mind. God knew that the animals left only to the male disposition might eventually be in serious trouble.

When the woman's disposition is not allowed expression in a culture or subculture, the environment will become more hardhearted. Many such cultures exist today, and in those cultures there is not the interest in peacemaking, malnutrition, diseases, etc., as there could be.

Not only do male and female need one another, but the world at large needs the balance. In fact, God's image is not bottled up and restricted in either male or female alone, but in both. God has reproduced something of His own nature in male and in female. Through the combination of both, God maintains the balance of conquering (male characteristic) and caring (female characteristic), of protecting (female characteristic) and penetrating (male characteristic). No wonder we read, "When God created man (humanity), He made him (corporate pronoun for humanity) in the likeness of God. He created them male and female, and He blessed them and named them (male and female) Man (humanity) in the day when they were created" (Genesis 5:1, 2).

As soon as God declared that He would make a helper suitable

23

for man, He surprised us. Instead of immediately making that helper, He organized the first Barnum and Bailey parade. He brought all the animals to Adam (Genesis 2:18-20). Why? Just to get some names? No, that wasn't the only reason. The last part of the text gives us a major reason, "But for Adam there was not found a helper suitable for him."

God was preparing Adam for what was coming up next. Adam saw that each animal had a mate. He also saw that none of them was suitable for himself. That's an important lesson for us to learn. No pet can take the place of your mate. So don't treat your pet better than your mate.

Fellows, when you come home from work, don't greet the dog, "Hi, Ginger, how are you old gal?" and pet and stroke the dog, and then walk right by the wife as if she is lifeless furniture. If you do that, no wonder the dog's tail wags and the wife's spirit drags when you hit the house.

A few years ago I was staying with a family that had a house dog. I learned a valuable lesson from them. That dog had the husband's car tuned-in. When the car got a half block from the house, the dog headed for the door. (So I've got some advice for you gals—beat the dog to the door and grab that man.)

After God eliminated animals as man's counterpart, He then acted as the first matchmaker. "So the Lord God caused a deep sleep to fall upon the man, and he slept; then he took one of his ribs, and closed up the flesh at that place. And the Lord God fashioned into a woman the rib which He had taken from the man, and brought her to the man" (Genesis 2:21, 22).

Some people say that she has been ribbing the man ever since, but that's not true, nor is it the significance of using man's rib. Jewish rabbis were the first to observe that God did not take woman from a bone of man's foot that he would step on her, nor from a bone of man's head that he would dominate over her; but He took her from a bone of man's rib, because that's where she belongs—next to his side, under his arm, close to his heart.

When Adam saw Eve, he was surely excited, and he exclaimed, "This at last," which was his way of saying, "Where have you been, Baby?" Howard Hendricks paraphrases Adam's first response with just one word—"Whoopee," followed by a whistle. Adam did not see Eve as a competitor, but as a companion. He didn't see her as property for using, but as a partner for sharing. He saw her as one with him, "This is now bone of my bones, and flesh of my flesh; she shall be called Woman, because she was taken out of Man."

Adam caught on immediately that husband and wife need each other. Part of what it means to love each other is to admit need of each other.

Following are some words that have become precious to me. I'll put my wife's name, Julia, into them. These words capture something of what God was communicating when He said, "It is not good for the man to be alone; I will make him a helper suitable for him."

Alone I am partial, I am not whole.
Alone you are partial, my darling,
    But you are not whole.
Together there is more.

I know some things, Julia, that
    you do not know.

But the things you know when shared with me
    make my mind richer.

I can do some things, sweetheart,
    that you cannot do.

But the kinds of things you can do
    when shared with me make my life
    so much more meaningful.

I have some interests that you do
    not have, my mate.

But the interests you have when
    shared with me make my world
    larger.

Oh, yes, Julia, together there is more,
    but just being together is not enough.

It's like sheep in need of a
    shepherd.

It's like branches in need of a
    vine.

It's like a body in need of a
    head.

Therefore, my darling wife,
    it is only in Jesus Christ—
    the Good Shepherd, the Vine,
    and the Head,
    that together your life and mine,
    shared with each other and for each other—
Together, we can become whole.

For Consideration or Discussion

1. For men only: How long has it been since you—
   Intentionally set aside some time to talk to your wife about how
   she is doing, how she is feeling, and what her hopes and dreams
   might be?
   Intentionally touched your wife with gentleness and affection at
   intervals through the day?
   Thanked your wife for her cooking, housework, and care of the
   children?
   Ran the sweeper, or did other household chores?
   Got up in the night to change and feed the baby?
   Presented your wife with a surprise gift?
   Passed on to your wife something nice others said about her?
   Told your wife you love her?
   Made a special effort to insure that your wife experiences as
   much satisfaction in lovemaking as you do?
   Gave your wife some cash to spend as she wishes?
2. For women only: How long has it been since you—
   Thanked your husband for the hard work he does for the fam-
   ily?
   Expressed appreciation for his good characteristics and strong
   points?
   Took the initiative in lovemaking?
   Gave him some space, such as your hearty support for some
   time spent with male companions doing something that is not in
   your line of interest?
   Surprised him with an unexpected gift?
   Said, "I am glad I married you"?

Three Factors for a Longer Marriage

3

Every time Jesus was asked about the longevity of marriage, part of His answer included Genesis 2:24 (Matthew 19:5; Mark 10:5-7). Evidently locked into this verse are the important concepts about marriage our Master wants us to adopt. They are easy to spot— leaving, cleaving, and becoming one flesh. ("For this cause a man shall leave his father and his mother, and shall cleave to his wife; and they shall become one flesh.")

One man has compared these three factors to a three-sided tent. One side of the tent is made of the fabric of leaving, one side of the fabric of cleaving, and one side of the fabric of oneness. When children are born into the family, guess where they are in relationship to that tent. You're right—they are on the inside of it. They are resting under the tent (for their protection, security, and development). But if there is a gap in any one of the sides, storms of the world can come pouring in to drown out some of that protection, security, and development.

Since these three factors are so important, and have to do with the relationship between husband and wife, let's take a look at what they mean and don't mean.

Leaving

"Leaving father and mother" has nothing to do with geographical location. It doesn't mean that we have to "split" and get a thousand miles away from home. In fact, when that was written, newly married couples lived close to home—very close. Parents would just add another room to the house and the married children would move in.

"Leaving" does not mean that we lose respect for our parents. Jesus quoted this verse to an adult audience. To the same kind of audience He said, "Honor your father and mother" (Matthew 15:4).

I'm going to share with you something that it took me forty years to get straight. In fact, I'm still working on it. Before I decided to study for the ministry, I was an air traffic controller at O'Hare Airport in Chicago (in the days before the union, slow down, strikes, and firing). I was a bachelor and did that kind of work for ten years, and I thoroughly loved it. When I went to southern Illinois to visit my mother, how did she see me? As a senior controller in the world's busiest airport? No, she saw me as her little boy. When we sat down to eat, she would say, "Son, don't you think you should finish the food on your plate?" Around Christmastime she would always say, "Son, are you sure that coat of yours is heavy enough for this weather?"

Now I'm married, have four children, have been a college professor, and am a college president. I have written twenty-two books. (This is number twenty-three.) I travel and speak all over the country. How does my mother see me now? You guessed it! I'm still her little boy. I was with her not long ago, and she was still trying to get me to eat oatmeal for breakfast.

Do you have any idea what that used to do to me? Of course you do, because you've been in the same boat. That smothering used to tear me up on the inside. I would try not to let mother know that I was ticked off, but I must have blown it many times. She could tell by the look on my face and the tone of my voice.

But when I was forty-years-old, I began to get my head on straight. I was looking at my children, and it dawned upon me that no matter what those kids become they will always be my boy and girls. If Randy should become the President of the United States, he will just be my little boy living in the White House. If that should happen, I have already decided what I will do. If I hear he is going to take a trip to the U.S.S.R. in the middle of the winter, I'm going to call him on the telephone—collect. I'm going to say, "Son, I've just one question—are you sure that coat of yours is heavy enough for the weather over there?"

I know it bugs you teenagers when your parents want you in at a certain hour. And if you don't make it home, they worry and may even call around. It's not because they don't trust *you*. It is everybody else who is out on the streets late at night that they don't trust. Is it *that* bad to have someone who loves you enough to care? If you have a pet dog who is not home when you get there, I suspect you go searching for him all over the neighborhood. *Your folks love you more than you love that dog.*

The moment you walk down an aisle, and stand next to the person you love and say "I do," are your folks sitting there thinking, "Whew, we got rid of that one—finally"? Nope! Now you may be thinking that, but not your folks. They have an attachment to you that continues. For instance, your mother has special kinds of attachment. Why you nearly kicked her to death before she ever saw the color of your eyes. And you literally made her sick— morning after morning after morning. In fact, those mornings turned into some *mournings*. You cannot remember, but your mother cannot forget.

There were many nights when your mother lost more sleep than you did (while your father was sleeping away, unaware anything was happening). Those were the nights when your body was hot with fever. Every time you turned over, your mother was awake. Many times she would hug your hot, limp, sick body close to her, and even wish and pray that the sickness could leave your body and infest hers. So the moment you say "I do," in no way is she whispering, "Good riddance."

"Leaving" father and mother does not mean we walk away from caring about them. Jesus and Paul made it clear that children have a responsibility to provide physically for their parents (Matthew 15:1-9; Mark 7:10-13; 1 Timothy 5:4). Jesus clearly connected providing for parents with honoring them. To be religious while neglecting parents makes void "the word of God" (Matthew 15:6). Paul said that whoever neglects his parents "has denied the faith, and is worse than an unbeliever" (1 Timothy 5:8). Children should not relinquish this care to some kind of governmental program. After all, the government did not care for you when you were growing up. So you shouldn't expect them to care for your parents when they grow old. Paul taught that parents should care for themselves when able to do so. But if they are not able, the children and grandchildren should provide the care. If these do not, the church should (1 Timothy 5:4-16).

If leaving mother and father doesn't mean we leave geographically, or in our respect or in our caring, then what does it mean? It means that we cut out the dependency (the apron strings). It means that when we marry someone, we realize that our parents have brought us to a certain level of development. We are thankful for that, but in God's plan the person we marry completes our development and maturity. We switch our dependency and submission from our parents to our married partner. Practically speaking, this means that neither the bride or bridegroom keeps running home or calling home to have their parents call the shots in the new family. It even means that neither person has to spend *every* Saturday or Sunday with the parents. (I know some marriages that are in continual hot water because every weekend belongs to the parents.) Too much is just too much. The dependency (umbilical) cord has to be cut.

Perhaps the toughest side is the parents' side. It's not easy to "let go," but we must. We need to give our children freedom to develop a new family unit just as someone gave us that freedom.

One mother told me about the wedding gift she gave her daughter-in-law on the day of her son's wedding. She gave her daughter-in-law a box full of her son's things that the mother had treasured—some trophies, ribbons, awards, etc. At the bottom of the box was a new apron with the strings cut off. On their tenth anniversary, the daughter-in-law thanked the mother again for the most meaningful gift she got on her wedding day—a new apron with the strings cut off. She also thanked her for living out that gift. In a sense, her mother-in-law was a continual gift by granting freedom.

Whether or not you will allow your children to leave father or mother partly depends upon how you see yourself and how you see your children. Do you see yourself as a controller or as a catalyst? Do you have poor or good self-esteem? Do you get your total feeling of worth from the fact that your children depend upon you? If so, you will be in trouble.

Although we leave our father and mother, we marry something of our in-laws whether we like it or not. Some of the life-style of the in-laws will move in with you, because your mate was reared in the environment of the in-laws. This can cause real stress. It's called *expectation gap,* and it works like this:

Jack's father never kissed his mother in front of the kids. That didn't mean he did not love her; he just didn't express it publicly. Jill was raised in a family where her father kissed her mother every time he left the house—even to get the morning paper from the lawn.

Jack's family never remembered birthdays or anniversaries. In fact, he didn't even know his folks' anniversary date. Jill's family made special occasions out of birthdays; her folks' anniversary was the biggest celebration of the year—only Christmas outdid it. On every anniversary, Jill's mother would prepare a candlelight dinner and have soft romantic music playing. She would meet her husband at the door, and his arms were full of packages.

So Jack and Jill marry each other. Soon after the honeymoon, Jack forgets to kiss Jill when he leaves for work. Guess what? Jill begins to think, "He's losing his love for me." By the time they've been married a year, Jack is consistent. Now he forgets to kiss her *every* day when he leaves for work.

Jill is crushed, but today is their anniversary. Today their marriage can get turned around. So Jill spends all day preparing a candlelight dinner. She meets Jack at the door, and what does he have in *his* arms—absolutely nothing. He has forgotten. Jill leads him into the dining room to see the candlelight dinner. Jack has seen only one candlelight dinner in his entire life. His mother had really goofed up one day, so, to keep Jack's dad from going through the ceiling, she prepared a candlelight dinner and manipulated him into a nonaggressive mood. Jack sees the candlelight dinner, thinks back to that first candlelight dinner, and yells, "What have you done wrong today, Jill? I know why all women prepare candlelight dinners." Then he blows out the candles. What a way to spend an anniversary together.

The difficulties of leaving mother and father are escalated by marrying something of the in-laws. The newly married couple needs to take time to adjust to each other. It can happen if each is committed not only to leaving but also to cleaving.

Cleaving

Without leaving there can be no cleaving. Leaving permits cleaving.

If a husband and wife do not cleave to each other, a vacuum will develop. Each will eventually develop a substitute to cleave to. It may be a job, a friend, a project, children, things, etc. Any substitute that comes between the cleaving of husband and wife weakens their relationship, threatens the security of their children, and delays the development that God intends to happen within a marriage.

The "cleave" used here is the strongest word in Hebrew for two things glued together. It is the super glue of Genesis. It means the opposite of withdrawing (2 Kings 18:6). It means a determined persistence to stick with a person (Deuteronomy 13:4; Ezekiel 29:4; Job 19:20; Psalms 22:15; 119:31; Jeremiah 13:11; Lamentations

4:4). Husband and wife should be so committed to each other that nothing is allowed to come between them—not a car, company, cult, club, career, or children. Sometimes it is easy to begin to live primarily for the children instead of for the mate. It is damaging to cling more to the children than to the married partner.

Dr. David Mace led a study to determine why children run away from home. The study considered the children's school activities, extracurricular activities, work habits, peer group, social life, and, of course, homelife. The study concluded that no group of factors appear to have influenced the runaways more powerfully than the relatively poor quality of the parents' marriages.

> All my experiences across the world (I have been involved in family programs in sixty countries) tell me that the best setting for the healthy development of a child is to have two parents who live together in a warm, close, mutually supportive relationship. This relationship is critical even if the parents lack money, or education, or sophistication.

Isn't that an amazing conclusion? Money, education, and sophistication make up the trinity so much of this nation is in a race to acquire. All of a sudden I'm understanding better how some of our parents, grandparents, and great-grandparents did such a good job of raising their children without the experts of today. They had good relationships with each other. Dr. Mace continued by saying, "There is no more precious gift we can bestow upon our children than to give them parents who care for and respect"—guess whom—"each other." To strive for such a marital relationship is an inescapable duty of every parent.

To cleave to each other means that we live *for* each other not just *with* each other. There is a big difference between living *with* someone and living *for* someone. We have mice that live *with* us, but they don't live *for* us—nor do we live *for* them.

Cleaving to each other primarily means commitment to each other. In modern talk, it means to do the "I dos" in those wedding vows. Do you remember those vows—For richer or for *poorer;* in health or in *sickness;* for better or for *worse.* And some of it is for poorer, sickness, and worse.

Some of it is for poorer. For years I heard that two people could live as cheaply as one. I started believing it—and then I got married.

I sold a new Buick for a stick-shift Chevy to afford marriage and a honeymoon. (I even thought it would be great to teach my new bride how to drive a stick shift on the honeymoon. What a dumb decision. It was a disaster.) I discovered something about economics on the honeymoon. People charged me *more* money for two in a motel room. When the ticket at restaurants arrived, the price was doubled. Later the insurance company wanted more money to insure my wife. Both of us were in college, and the tuition was double what I had been paying for myself. For our last year of college, we used insurance money for our damaged car to pay bills. We were the only students in college with a car minus two fenders and a grill. Five years later, we broke our son's piggy bank in order to get money to buy baby formula for him. *It's sometimes for poorer.*

Some of it is also for sickness. I did not marry until I was twenty-nine. By that time I had some criteria I wanted in a wife. One criterion was this—I didn't want to marry a sickly woman and spend the rest of my life holding hands with someone in a hospital. I now realize how immature that criterion was. I have since met many people who are sick most of the time, and they are some of the most delightful, helpful, and wonderful people I have ever known. Nevertheless, that was a criterion of mine.

On about the third date I had with Julia, I realized I could fall in love with her. (Whatever "fall in love" means.) So I made it a point on that date to drive by the Lincoln Memorial Hospital in Lincoln, Illinois. (The Lincoln Memorial Hospital is not on the way to any-where.)

As we drove by, I said, "Julia, I wonder what it is like to be a patient in a hospital like that."

"I don't know," she said.

It wasn't enough input for me, so I tried again.

"Well, haven't you ever been sick in the hospital?"

"Not since I was born."

That didn't quite do it either.

"Well, don't you get sick very often?"

This was really an exciting conversation for a date.

"Hardly ever," she quickly replied.

Within seven months I married her. We took a seven-day hon-eymoon through the Smoky Mountains; the last two days she was sick *in the hospital.* In fact, she got sick at the end of our first full day. Sick *twice* in seven days. I began to wonder about everything else she had told me during our courting days. But she hasn't been in the hospital since—except when the children were born. *Some of it is for sickness.*

People cannot stay married on feeling alone in our pressure-cooker society. There are days you don't feel good about your mate or yourself. There are days you feel like saying, "I made a mistake." There are days you don't feel like saying to your mate, "I like you," let alone, "Baby, I *adore* you!"

Some of it is for worse. A young couple, who have three children under three years of age, and two of them still in diapers, would be a good example. The children have had diarrhea all day. When the husband comes home from work, and opens the door to the living room, he smells something. He knows it's not dinner.

He doesn't know it, but his wife has had the flu all day. When he gets inside, she says, "Honey, I'm sick in bed. Timmy and Tommy are sick, and Tommy needs his diaper changed. Could you do that for me?" (Do you know what I've discovered about maleness? It's a model of a macho he-man to shovel that stuff out of the barn on a farm, but one little bitty diaper wipes us out.) Just as he gets Tommy all cleaned up, and with his hand underneath his bare bottom, it's time for diarrhea *all over* again. He runs into the bedroom in a panic and says, "Honey, help!" and she vomits all over him. There's just no way in the world that *feeling* will get you through such times. It has to be *commitment.* That's cleaving.

One Flesh

The third factor is "one flesh." But what in the world does that mean? The one-flesh concept has two meanings. It refers to the physical consummation of a marriage. In that love-act is a communication of unity. The minds are united (or should be), the emotions are united (or should be), the purpose is united (or should be), the communication that comes through this act is united (or should be), and the bodies are united.

The physical act of love should be a crowning experience of the leaving and cleaving that has preceded it. A satisfyingly meaningful sex life does not begin by how two people get into bed at night. Rather it begins by how they get out of bed in the morning, and their interpersonal relationship with each other all day. It's an escalated "I love you" that reinforces all the other "I love yous" that have been going on.

This dimension of "one flesh" can be perverted when it is entered into without the prerequisites of the leaving and cleaving. Then the "one flesh" act is out of place. Paul spotlighted it in 1 Corinthians 6. Just because a "one-flesh" act has happened doesn't mean two people are married. That can be sheer adultery.

The second meaning of "one flesh" goes beyond the physical relationship. It encompasses the holistic relationship of two people. This meaning of "one flesh" certainly doesn't mean numerically one. (I am writing this chapter on Air Canada Airlines, 37,000 feet in the air. My wife is in her body 600 miles ahead and 37,000 feet below. Right now I'm riding in a plane toward the airport. She's driving a car toward the airport. We are in two separate bodies.)

While "one" doesn't mean numerically one, it does mean a unit—a team. Julia and I can be 600 miles apart horizontally, 37,000 feet apart vertically, and still be one team. Jesus emphasized this meaning of "one flesh" immediately after quoting Genesis 2:24. He said, "What therefore God has joined together, let no man separate" (Matthew 19:6). The word Jesus used for "joined" is the Greek word for "yoke." When two are put into the same yoke, they keep their own personalities and bodies, but they become a single team. They become two who live side by side as cooperating and complementary companions; who share the same purposes, goals, values, and life-styles. The unit should be so tight that each person acts in the absence of the other as he would if the other were present. (I am away from home much of the time, but I know that my wife will make the kinds of decisions she would have made were I present. Our goals are the same. I trust her because of our mutuality.)

Our commonness of goals is partly due to the fact that we worked them out together. Our goals are higher than either of us individually, or both of us collectively. We have both adopted God's goals as revealed in His Word for ourselves and our children. Consequently, our goals do not change with the shifting sand. A person who doesn't know the harbor he wants will set his sail to any wind that blows. That brings insecurity to the relationship of a husband and wife. Neither should have to second-guess what will please the other. Husbands and wives should not have to play games with each other.

The sequence of leaving, cleaving, and becoming one flesh is important for a stable marriage, but the more important factor is the purpose each partner has for life.

If the goal is stable, the leaving will be settled, the cleaving will be secure, and the unity will be sweet. Too many marriages have broken up because of the lack of a harmonious purpose for living. Without a harmonious purpose, married partners become more open to cleaving to a substitute than to the other partner.

We are learning that the most important motivating factor for actions is the future goal a person keeps in focus. A shift of goals in the unit causes weakness and problems. Separate goals can allow agreement, cooperation, and trust to cave in to disagreement, competition, and doubt.

I know some people may say, "I've already goofed. I'm divorced, or divorced and remarried. I feel like I've come to an end." But that is not an unforgivable situation. Our God has never been in the business of locking people up to their past blunders or experiences. Some people seem to be in that business, and they seem to enjoy it. They aren't getting their cues from God.

God has always been in the business of releasing people from their past, of picking up the broken pieces of humanity and putting them into a beautiful mosaic—much like a stained-glass window with many irregular and jagged edges. What a beautiful sight when the light of the sun shines through! And so it is with broken people. What a beautiful sight they become when the light of the Son shines through!

In 1929, Southern Cal was playing Georgia Tech in the Rose Bowl. Just before halftime, Ray Rigels got the ball for Southern Cal. In the excitement of the Rose Bowl, he started running in the wrong direction and toward the wrong goalposts. One of his own teammates tackled him just before touchdown. Georgia Tech got the ball. There was time for only one play before halftime, and Georgia Tech made the touchdown.

People in the stands wondered whether or not Ray Rigels would ever play in that game again. Down in the dressing room, just before halftime ended, the coach said, "The boys who started the first half also start the second half." Ray had been one of the starters. The players began to run out on the field. But not Ray. He just sat on the bench with his head in his hands. He was paralyzed by his past blunder. The coach said, "Ray, did you hear me? You're playing. Let's go!"

But Ray just sat there in the self-made concrete of his past experience. The coach walked up to him and said, "Ray, get up and get back on that field. This game is not over. I'll be with you."

That's the way our God is with us. You may have run in the

wrong direction. You may have really goofed it in your relationship with your mate—and even known better. I have. But our God says, "Get up, and get back into living. Life is not over, and I'll be with you." Our God specializes in forgiveness. He's the Master at mending lives.

On a recent weekend I stayed in the room of my hosts' son. On his wall he had a poster that I had never seen before. The poster had a stream that kept getting narrower. It finally made a small bend and looked as if it had dried up completely. But a bit beyond what looked like the end was a fantastically beautiful large body of water. The words on that poster captured what God loves to do in our lives: "What appears to be the end may really be a new beginning."

Have you reached what appears to be the end? Do the days ahead of you look closed and locked? Then get ready. You may be on the verge of a new beginning. God specializes in new beginnings.

For Consideration or Discussion

1. Share with the group what it was like for you to leave home.
2. Were you sufficiently independent of your family when you married? Was that a problem? Does it continue to be a problem in your marriage?
3. How did you go about the business of becoming independent from your family, a person in your own right?
4. If you are a parent, are you planning to work yourself out of a job by teaching your growing children to gradually become more independent? What is your plan for reaching your objective?
5. Once a parent, always a parent. Agree _____ Disagree _____
   Parenting is not over when a child reaches eighteen. Agree _____ Disagree _____
   Parenting of a seventeen-year-old is a little different from the parenting of a fifteen-year-old. Agree _____ Disagree _____
   (If you checked "agree" on the above items, you are in disagreement with most authorities on family life.)
6. If you have blundered in a past relationship, ask God to forgive you and believe that He will. "God has never been in the business of locking people up to their past blunders or experiences."

Love
and Marriage
4

Love and marriage, love and marriage,
Go together like a horse and carriage.
Dad was told by mother,
"You can't have one without the other."

That's a great idea, but it isn't true. You *can* have love without having marriage. We cannot marry every person of the opposite sex whom we love.

It's also possible to have marriage without love. In fact, that is the norm in many cultures where the marriages are arranged by the parents. Sometimes the bride and groom do not even meet until the day of the wedding. They may know about each other without knowing each other. Isaac and Rebekah experienced that type of marital beginning (Genesis 24).

In our culture we tend to think "that kind of marriage will never work," but those marriages last longer than ours. A man from one of those cultures recently told me that there has not been a divorce in the last five hundred years in his native culture. People in his culture do not "fall in love" first, and then marry because they love each other. They get married with the commitment to learn to love the other person because they are now married.

There is nothing in the Bible that says we must love first and then marry. But there is a lot in the Bible that says we are to love and respect the person we marry. In fact, we are told that older women are to teach younger women how to love their husbands (Titus 2:3, 4).

Rather than love being the proper environment for marriage to grow, marriage is the proper environment for love to develop.

Although love may not always lead to marriage, marriage should always lead to love. Love does not automatically create a new husband-wife unit. But a husband-wife unit, created by a marriage that involves leaving, cleaving, and unity, creates the environment in which love can flourish. If it doesn't, don't blame the other person. Love is something you do—not a *reaction* to another person's actions.

We can compare this to children being born into a family. We did not fall in love with them first and then allow them to become a part of the family. It wasn't "I love you. Will you be my child?" Oh no! It is "I love you because you are my child." It was their entrance into our family that cranked out our love for them. The same children born into another family would not draw out the same kind of love from us. It's our family commitment to them that matures our love for them—not their looks, their abilities, their personalities, etc. Many days they disappoint us and cause us to want to climb the walls. Many days they don't feel good about us, and we don't feel good about them. But we don't run straight to the courts and file parent-child divorce proceedings. Why? Because our family commitment provides the environment for love to grow in spite of disappointments, hurts, littleness, etc. They belong to us, and we are going to keep loving them. That means we have to develop such attitudes and actions as patience, understanding, forgiveness, longsuffering (and sometimes it can really be long), gentleness, self-control, kindness. We don't keep score of the times we've been hurt by them. We learn to bury bitterness and wrath. We also learn to discipline. We learn to give them freedom with trust. All of this is tough. But it is love. We don't do these things because we always feel like it, or because we think the children always deserve it, or because they are loving us back. We do it because we are tied to them by a family connection.

This is also the way it should be between husband and wife in a marriage. They are tied together by a marriage connection. The Bible considers marriage to be a covenant between two people. It calls for both of them to work hard at living out that covenant with faithfulness and responsibility. Lack of feeling does not break the covenant. So it does not break our commitment to love.

Our marriage vows do not read, "Until my feeling for you dies out." But a lot of people seem to interpret them that way. Some couples say, "We want to dissolve our marriage because our chemistry for each other has changed." They need to change their chemistry, not their mates. How do they do that? Well, they don't do it by letting their emotions control their actions. At the time they feel least like doing some loving act for their mate is the time when they may need to do it most. Actions do not always follow emotions. Many times emotions follow actions.

The more good you do for someone, the more good you will feel about that person. Act lovely so that lovely emotions can catch up with your actions. Lovely actions cannot only change you; they can also change your mate. It may take time (much time), but a long-term marriage can be worth it. You can't be changing partners every time your feelings take a dive. There are many reasons why feelings go into a tailspin—physical changes, job stress, economical disappointments, food intake, air pressures, certain periods of the month, certain cycles (or passages) in a person's life, etc. A tailspin does not have to lead to a crash or a bailout. However, it is true that we can surely become nauseated about the whole thing while the tailspin is happening.

Why is it that so often "love" seems to fail to sustain a marriage? One reason may be that our society does not encourage couples to make a binding, unconditional commitment to each other. We are prone to stress independence, autonomy, individualism, and freedom rather than interdependence, community, or a corporate personality. Also there are other factors: the insecurity of our high mobility, the looseness of sexual expression prior to and outside of marriage, the lack of interpersonal sharing, the glorification of freedom from marriage commitments as the fun thing to do (communicated through TV programs and movies), the lack of models at home, the stress on the "me" mentality, the "pull your own strings" and "look out for number one" philosophy, the lack of trust in people (which leads us to jealousy and causes us to be threatened if our mate is making friends and maturing in his/her personality or relationships with others), the tendency to develop separate interests and potentialities (which can eventually lead to a low self-image out of which love has a difficult time growing), the failure to let the past be the past, etc.

One of the main reasons marriage does not survive the "fall in love first and then get married" schedule is that we have not done a very good job of learning what kind of love it takes for marriage.

We use the same little four-letter word (love) for all kinds of different loves. For instance, a man can say, "I love my wife" or "I love my car." He has a different kind of love in mind (or he should). What happens when his car gets old and starts wearing out? He goes car shopping. If his love for his wife is no different, then what happens when she gets older and starts—well, gets older? He may go wife shopping.

A car doesn't even have to get old before a man starts looking for another one. (I once bought a new car that I kept just three weeks before I traded it in. It was a beauty of a car. Heads turned when I drove it. But I just didn't like the way it handled at high speeds. Those were the days when the only speed limit in Illinois was "reasonable and proper," and any speed was reasonable and proper as long as the car was under control.) I've known some marriages that didn't last even three weeks.

If we are determined to fall in love first, and get married because we love each other, then we'd better learn a bit more about love.

I've done a bit of premarital counseling. In the first sessions I always ask, "Why do you want to get married?" I've never had a couple say, "Because we hate each other." It's always, "Because we love each other."

I then ask, "How do you know you do?"

It's interesting to watch their faces. It's as if a wet rag had just smacked them across the cheek. What was a delightful glow just seconds before often turns into a dull glare. I usually get the impression that each one is inwardly asking, "How *do* I know?" Then after a significant pause, the answer is usually, "We like to be together."

Isn't that nice? I used to have a dog, and we just loved to be together. But I never thought about marriage. Another classic answer is, "We have similar interests." Great! My mother-in-law and I have similar interests.

It's one thing to like to be with someone with similar interests for periods of time when most of the conditions are favorably planned and executed. But it is quite another ball game to live with someone when the paycheck stops, the baby's crying will not, the plumbing is frozen, the wife has missed two menstrual periods (and the youngest child is graduating from high school), you've just discovered that your mate is or has had an affair, etc.

How can two people know in advance that their love will survive such crises? There is never one hundred percent proof that it will. But there are certain levels of love that we know cannot survive them. And there is one level of love that can. The question is: Which level of love do you intend to have when you walk down the aisle? Which level of love do you have now?

Levels of Love

There are three different levels of love that a person can have when he marries. The truth is that all of us have each of these levels of love in our lives in some degree or another. We need to be asking ourselves, "Which level of love am I demonstrating in this situation?" While each of us has all three of these loves, one level of love is dominant. The Greeks called these three levels *eros, philos,* and *agape.*

Eros is always one-way love—back to self. It is selfish love. Some people teach that *eros* love is always sexual love, but that is not accurate. In fact, the Greek word for sexual love between a husband and wife in the Old Testament was agape. (See Genesis 24:67.)

Eros love looks out for number one. It doesn't care how much the other person is inconvenienced, just as long as self is being fulfilled. It is babyish love. Some have described *eros* love like this: "I love you *if* or *as long as* I get my way." Love of this kind can never keep people together. In fact, the Greek word for strife came from the root for *eros.*

Eros love is headed for strife, not stability. *Eros* love enters into a marriage with the determination to remain married only as long as things go well—meaning, "go my way." Run fast from *eros* love. Don't think you can change it into a different kind of love after marriage. *Eros* love can be changed; but a person dominated by selfish love will not remain with you in a marriage long enough for the change to take place.

People who date can spot *eros* love easily if they look for it. Does he always have to have his way? Is he kind? Is he patient? Does he ever say, "If you love me, you will do thus and so?" When he says, "If you love me, you will let me" that is your clue. He loves self not you.

Philos love is the "mutual admiration society" kind of love. It is the love between close friends. Think now of your closest friends. That's *philos* love. It is always two-way love. You are contributing something to your friend's life, and your friend is contributing something to your life.

As beautiful as this love is, it is not the love that can keep a marriage going. Although husbands and wives need to be friends, they need a love that goes beyond just friendship love.

With *philos* love, as soon as one person quits contributing to the friendship it is broken. Oh, you may still like each other, but the two of you are no longer the kind of friends that are contributing to each other's lives. That's one reason we change friends as life goes on.

Philos love is the "I love you because of" love. There is a reason for our attraction to that other person. It may be his looks, his personality, his intelligence, his athletic abilities, etc.

Some people get married with *philos* love as the dominant love. It is easy to do, especially for teenagers. I fell in and out of love every three weeks while I was in high school. Probably one reason I never gained weight in high school was because I was always lovesick. I was either lovesick because of a "new love," or lovesick because I had just lost the dream of my life—every three weeks. More than likely I would have married any one of them if she had just popped the question. I didn't know it then, but I know it now—I was developing friendships, not wives. We cannot marry all our friends, but the person we marry should be our friend (if we live in a culture where we love first and then marry). However, the love to marry on needs to be a level beyond *philos* love.

The "I love you because of" will not keep two people together for several reasons: (1) People can lose their "becauses." "I love you because you are beautiful." There is nothing wrong with being attracted by beauty. But if the love does not progress beyond beauty, what happens when a Mack truck hits her in the face? "I love you because you are athletic." Good! Nothing wrong with wanting someone with whom to do sports. But what happens to the love if he loses a leg or becomes paralyzed from the waist down? People can lose their "becauses." (2) People can come along with better "becauses." What happens when someone else shows up who makes your beauty queen look like Frankenstein's identical twin? What happens when you meet someone else whose athletic abilities makes your "star" look as if he's working toward a PhD in clumsiness?

Philos love can also foster suspicion, feelings of inferiority and insecurity within a marriage. If a girl knows her husband married her just because of her beauty, she may begin to worry and distrust him when she learns that a more beautiful girl works near him. Love of this kind can also foster dishonesty in relationships. If you realize that someone loves you because of a certain characteristic, you may never allow him to see other traits of your peronality for fear he will not like you then. That kind of game-playing keeps a lot of people from being transparent. Unless you are transparent, you never allow the other person to love the real you, only a part of you, the mask you wear. Marriage has a way of taking off masks. Sometimes what is seen behind the mask is not the person who walked down the aisle. The just-because-of love is too fickle by itself to support a marriage.

Agape love is one-way love. It is always to and for the other person. It sees the needs of another, and it moves to meet those needs. It doesn't count the cost. It doesn't calculate what it will get in return. It doesn't consider whether or not the other person deserves it. The real issue is not, "Does he deserve it?" but, "Does he need it?" The other person *always* deserves it.

This is the "I love you in spite of" level of love. Coupled with *philos* it says, "There are reasons I have fallen in love with you. But now my love has grown beyond those reasons. If those reasons should no longer exist, I will still love you because I have grown to love the *total* you, not just the part of you that initially attracted me to you."

Another attitude-activity checklist on this can be found in Ephesians 4:22—5:33. Here are some of the items on that list:
Put away falsehood.

Speak the truth to one another. Husbands and wives need to be open with each other. Neither one can really know the other if either one wears a mask. Truthfulness is related to one's being trustworthy. If you want your husband or wife to trust you, be truthful.
Be angry, but do not sin. Do not let the sun set upon your anger.

The husband and wife need to communicate their differences. Anger over any issue should not be carried over to the next day. Never! If it is, the devil will take advantage of it by bringing disunity into the home. That is why Paul immediately says, "And do not give the devil an opportunity" (v. 27).
Do not steal from each other.

Both husband and wife should contribute their energies to the livelihood of the family, according to the roles of each. Each one should recognize how the other is needed for the family. Neither should be lazy and sponge off the other.
Mind your tongue.

Speech should build up each other; therefore speak well of each other and to each other. Replace slander with kindness. Remember that belittling each other whittles away the cleaving relationship. Words affect the total being of a person. Careless or unkind words can break a person's spirit and even his health; kind and encourag-

44

ing words can build up (Proverbs 12:18). Our speech at home should help maintain the unity at home.
Mind your attitude.

Grudges and bitterness should be replaced with forgiveness. A willingness to talk over grievances and work out difficulties will go far to replace attitudes of sullenness, bad temper, and stubbornness. Some say, "I'll forgive, but I won't forget." Deciding to remember hampers forgiveness and keeps grudges just around the corner. A person must develop the ability to forget. You can forget anything you want to forget. Merely forgetting, however, is not necessarily forgiving. Forgetting may not be a positive activity, but a neglectful one. Forgetting calls for no mutual reacceptance of one another. Only when the offender and the one offended together condemn the wrong, decide to forget it, and walk together without hostility, does forgiveness take place. Then alienation of a couple is replaced by reconciliation.

Agape love is the only kind of love that will motivate repentance when one mate hurts another and motivate forgiveness when a mate is hurt.

Not one of us is perfect. Be careful! Do not think that you married a perfect person. You did not. Neither did your mate marry a perfect person. In our imperfection we disappoint each other, discourage each other, and depress each other. When we do this, we need to repent. We need to repent when we neglect our mate; when we nitpick; when we are too judgmental and too critical; when we do not trust; when we sin against our mate.

Repentance needs to be met with forgiveness. The Holy Spirit is in us so the fruit of the Spirit can grow in our lives when things go sour. The fruit of the Spirit is always for the benefit of the other person who has hurt us. The first characteristic of that fruit is *agape* love. Every other characteristic flows out of that love. It should be expressed when that other person disappoints us. Even joy is for the other person's good. The angels in Heaven rejoice when one sinner repents. And a person should rejoice when his mate repents of a sin against him. That doesn't mean that the pain will go away. It doesn't mean all the scars will vanish over night. It does mean that we understand that every person is vulnerable to sin. No one is perfect. We rejoice when the person we love repents.

Peace, patience, kindness, goodness, faithfulness, gentleness, and self-control are all because of and for the other person. If the person we lived with were perfect, we would not need these charac-

45

teristics. All of them come from *agape* love. It is the only love that can cement a marriage until "death do us part."

Agape love is not easy, but it is essential. It is the love of God for us—and the love of God through us. Only with *agape* love do we become more and more like our Father who is in Heaven. Only then do we bring a bit of Heaven to earth. Only then does Heaven help the home.

These words from an unknown author, which I've adapted and added to, should be the kind of words husbands and wives say to each other—and mean them.

> I love you
> Not only for what you are,
> But for what I am
> When I am with you.
>
> I love you
> Not only for what
> You have made of yourself,
> But for what
> You are making of me.
>
> I love you
> For not being a perfectionist
> And nit-picking at
> Every flaw you see.
> I love you
> For the part of me
> That you bring out.
> I love you
> For putting your hand
> Into my heaped-up heart
> And passing over
> All the foolish, weak things
> That you can't help
> Dimly seeing there.
>
> And for drawing out
> Into the light
> All the beautiful belongings
> That no one else had looked
> Quite far enough to find.

I love you
For forgiving me
All of those things
That others would say you shouldn't.

I love you because you
Are helping me to make
Of the lumber of my life
Not a tavern
But a temple—
Out of the works
Of my every day
Not a reproach
But a song.

I love you
Because you are you
And you help me
To be a better me.

For Consideration or Discussion

How can we gauge whether or not it is *agape* love that dominates us? There are some Biblical checklists that we ought to run through from time to time. See 1 Corinthians 13:4-7. Instead of saying "Love is," say "I am."

I am patient . . . . Am I?
I am kind . . . . Am I?
I am not jealous . . . . Am I?
I do not brag . . . . Do I?
I am not arrogant . . . . Am I?
I am not rude . . . . Am I?
I do not have to have my way . . . . Do I?
I am not easily ticked off . . . . Am I?
I do not keep score when I'm hurt . . . . Do I?
I do not rejoice when I catch him in the wrong . . Do I?
I rejoice when he's right . . . . Do I?
I protect him . . . . Do I?
I believe him . . . . Do I?
I stay positive . . . . Do I?
I never give up . . . . Do I?

Mutual Submission

5

Ever wonder what a happy family is like? Modern research on families spends more time looking into families in trouble than families that are not in trouble. Consequently, we read more about negative things to avoid than positive things to embrace. However, there are *some* clues about what happy families are like. Dr. Nicholas Stinnett of Oklahoma State University recently completed a study of nearly one hundred families who were selected for cohesiveness, durability, and affection. Where there were differences among these families, each shared four important qualities:

1. Members frequently and spontaneously showed appreciation for each other.
2. Members communicated easily with each other. They openly faced conflicts rather than hid them. They sought out mutual solutions rather than each member claiming to be "in the right."
3. They had a high degree of spiritual unity, and they shared common values and goals.
4. They did a lot of things together.

Other studies reveal that members in successful families share such qualities as being allies not competitors to each other; they tolerate individual differences with an absence of rigidity; they are flexible in making adjustments and open to change.

Families with these characteristics are not just "born that way." It takes work and modeling. Primarily, it calls for the husband and wife to work hard at their marriage. Then they can model positive relationships with each other from which other family members can learn.

Paul talked about husband/wife relationships in the fifth chapter of Ephesians. Normally we like to begin reading the husband/wife section with verse 22, "Wives, be subject to your own husbands, as to the Lord." However, the section really begins with verse 21 which reads, "And be subject to one another in the fear of Christ." It teaches us that submission is not the exclusive role of the wife. Instead, submission is mutual. Husbands and wives are to submit to each other.

The words "be subject" in verse 22 do not really appear in the Greek. The verse literally reads, "Wives, to your husbands, as to the Lord." English editors have added the words "be subject." That's why the words are italicized in most translations. If they are left out, it doesn't mean that wives are not to be subject to their husbands. What wives are to do in verse 22 is drawn from what each is doing in verse 21. "Be subject to one another . . . wives to your own husbands."

Mutual submission does not allow dictatorship; nor does it allow us to continue to say that marriage is on the fifty-fifty basis. Anyone who tries to keep a marriage going on the fifty-fifty basis is in for trouble with a capital "T." (That rhymes with "P," and stands for Problems.) If we are willing to meet our mate only halfway, we may never meet him on any issue. Each person often has a different idea about where the halfway line is. If you miss the line by one-millionth of an inch, you miss really touching the other person. Deciding ahead of time where the line is sets up a line of demarcation. Then the fifty-fifty marriage sounds too much like a football game. We meet on the fifty-yard line (if we can find it). One person may be on the twenty-yard line, thinking that's the halfway point, while the other person is on the seventy-yard line. Then we back off and start kicking each other around like a football. No wonder we often fumble, pass the ball of blame without handling it ourselves, tackle each other, and yell "penalty."

Marriage is not fifty-fifty, but one hundred-one hundred. That's what submit to one another means. It means we go all the way to meet the needs of each other. When that happens, we will meet each other. Sometimes it may be on the "fifty-yard line," but usually not. There are times we need to go to the ninety-yard line. But we meet—with open arms, not with clenched fists. And we don't keep score about how far we had to go.

Submission is not a dirty word. It is a great word, for it describes the character of Jesus. No one was more submissive than He. But what does submission mean? It doesn't mean involuntary, blind obedience. It means the voluntary willingness to give up some self-interests for the well-being of others. Here are some aspects of submission from Philippians 2:3-7:

1. Do nothing from selfishness.
2. Do nothing from empty conceit.
3. Regard the other as more important than self.
4. Look out for the interest of the other.
5. Empty self.
6. Become a servant of the other.

The Greek word for submission literally means to "place under" another. But it doesn't mean as an inferior person. It means to "place under" the other as a supporter of that person; to be like pillars holding up a building. To submit to one another is to really care for each other. There are two beautiful descriptions of submission in the Bible. The description of a wife's submission is found in Proverbs 31:12. "She does him good and not evil all the days of her life." The description of a husband's submission is found in Ephesians 5:25. "Husbands, love your wives, just as Christ also loved the church and gave Himself up for her."

James Kenny wrote a delightful description of mutal submission (Copyright November 1978, St. Meinrad Archabby. Reprinted from *Marriage & Family Living* magazine):

> I was hungry and you fixed my dinner
> Naked and you washed my clothes
> Poor and you worked hard to bring
>   home a paycheck
> In darkness and you fixed the fuse
> Flooded and you got the plumber
> Sad and you put on a Judy Collins record
> Angry and you told a funny story
> Sick and you kept the kids quiet
> Desirous and you made love with me.

Isn't it easy to forget that taking care on the daily needs of each other is a ministry not only to our spouses but also to Jesus: Inasmuch as you did this to the least of these, you did it to Me. Family living is engaging in a special ministry to those who are close to us. There we get the on-the-job training that equips us well to minister to those who are at a distance from us. Living in the family prepares us to live in the world.

Submission is not a male-chauvinist word reserved for what the women are to do. Jesus submitted to God's will (1 Corinthians 15:28; Philippians 2:5-8). We are *all* to submit to God and His commands (James 4:7). *All* in the church are to be subject to Christ (Ephesians 5:24). We are *all* to submit to higher authorities in the community and nation (Romans 13:1-5). We are *all* to submit to the leaders of the church (Hebrews 13:17).

In the daily routine of living we submit. We submit to others at work, to cars on the highway, to people in shopping lines, children to parents, parents to children, etc.

There is no way we can develop into more mature people, and help others develop, if each of us lives only to "pull our own strings." Life is a battleground with wars to be won and persons to conquer. People become targets for manipulation instead of persons to value. Confusion, loneliness, pain, resentment, unhappiness, and dissatisfaction result.

The submissive person is a humble person who can yield, adapt, care, and reach out to another. He does not demand his rights and take off to do his own thing in disregard of another's needs. Mutual submission calls for us to yield the right-of-way at home. (My wife and I have different natures. I hate cold weather, but I don't mind the heat. She is the opposite. Cold invigorates her, but heat destroys her. So we have a different opinion about using the air conditioner in the summer. I see no need for having it on—after all, just look at that electric bill—but I submit to her needs—after all, they're hard to miss when she's dripping with perspiration and has a headache.)

I like no lights on unless someone is in that room. I spent the first seventeen years of married life following everyone around and turning off the lights or yelling "turn off the light." Since I am the only person in our house who was raised during the depression, I've finally decided I'm in a losing battle. I no longer go looking for unused lights. (I'll admit, though, I've been slow with this one.)

Julia was raised to believe it was a man's job to take out the garbage. I *hate* to take out the garbage. So guess who does it—our son! But before he got big enough, Julia yielded without a word of complaint.

We did not lose our rights when we got married, but we are learning to lose the need to demand them. That's part of mutual submission. As we do this, we also learn the art of mutually developing each other.

Nothing enhances personal development more than mutual

submission. Julia and I have developed new interests as a result of mutual submission. She gave me her love for western music. (I now wear western boots exclusively.) I gave her my love for the classical.

I gave her my love for travel. Until we married, she had not been more than two hundred miles away from home. I had traveled over most of the United States and many foreign countries. Now she loves to travel. We are looking forward to the time when we can do more of it together.

She gave me her love for stability. She likes a house to care for and live in. Now I have a harder time than she when moving from a place that we've put some work into.

She gave me her devaluation of material things, such as cars. I liked to drive new cars. (I bought two new ones the year before we got married.) But Julia had never had a new car in her family. We have had only two new cars in twenty years. (And they had an average of 125,000 miles when we got rid of them.) It's great not having car payments.

She gave me her interest in such "boring" things as PTA. I went only because she went. Eventually I became the president and planned the carnival—and I loved it.

We gave to each other four children. They have given to us many things neither of us had to give to each other. For instance, they have given to us a love for athletics. Formerly neither of us would have spent one hour at a ball park. But our kids have stretched us. We now spend a large chunk of every summer at ball parks. We even have family basketball, volleyball, baseball, and of all things, football games.

Mutual submissiveness involves doing the "one anothers" in the Bible. Each married couple can check up on how well he/she contributes to their mutuality by evaluating whether or not he/she is doing the following:

1. Being devoted to the other one
2. Giving preference to the other one
3. Loving the other one
4. Not condemning the other one
5. Building up the other one
6. Accepting the other one
7. Communicating with the other one
8. Being able to admonish the other without animosity
9. Serving the other one

10. Not biting and devouring the other one
11. Not envying the other one
12. Not provoking the other one
13. Bearing the other's burdens
14. Putting up with the other one
15. Being kind to the other one
16. Not lying to the other one
17. Forgiving the other one
18. Supporting the other one
19. Encouraging the other one
20. Not speaking evil about the other one
21. Not begrudging the other one
22. Admitting faults to the other one
23. Praying for the other one

Whatever you give to the other one, you give to yourself as well.

For Consideration or Discussion

1. For your private meditation:
   Do your family members show appreciation for each other?
   Do your family members openly face conflicts rather than evade them?
   Does your family share common values?
   Are your family members allies rather than competitors?
2. If the answer is "no" to these three questions, are you willing to be the first person in your family to change these behaviors?
3. Go ahead and make those changes for six weeks. Then record any positive corresponding changes in your family members.
4. If your family members failed to change, was it worth it for you to change? Check yourself on the "other ones" previously listed.

Introducing
Family Roles
6

How many members are in a Christian family? A Christian family has a minimum of three: God, the husband, and the wife. It has a maximum of five different categories of members: God, relatives who live in, children, the husband, and the wife. Each of these has a specific role to be expressed within the family.

God in the Family

God instituted the family unit as an expression of His love for us. Because He knew what man needed for his greatest good and pleasure, God provided the means to meet that need. The family is one of God's special provisions for man. Long before we heard it from sociologists, we read it in the Bible: The family is man's primary group for fulfilling his basic needs and providing the environment for his development as a personality.

One of God's revelations about the family is that He is to have first place in the home. Respect for God is listed at the head of the Ten Commandments. Jesus reemphasized this by saying, "He who loves son or daughter more than Me is not worthy of Me" (Matthew 10:37). In Luke 14:26, He said the same thing in another way: "If anyone comes to Me, and does not hate his own father and mother and wife and children and brothers and sisters, yes, and even his own life, he cannot be My disciple." Jesus was not speaking harshly. He did not contradict himself. He did not say that we should despise family members or ourselves, for He also taught that we should honor father and mother (Matthew 15:4-6), and have a cleaving relationship with the marriage partner (Matthew 19:5). He also made it clear that we are to love each other (Matthew 22:39).

Jesus certainly did not contradict himself, but He gave us priorities by which we can love others properly.

The Greek word for "hate" in Luke 14:26 means to give someone second place. Jesus said that we should put our love for family members beneath our love for Him. As we share our love first with God, He will share His love with us. It is as His love abides in us that we are better able to love others (John 15; Romans 5:5; 1 John 4:16). He who abides in love abides in God (1 John 4:16). Although love begins with God, it cannot end there (1 John 4:21).

If we bypass or neglect devotion and love to God in order to show more love for the family, we will deplete our love capacity. Love that puts God anywhere but in first place will not last through wealth and poverty, sickness and health, agreements and disagreements. Only when God is the honored guest in our homes will the home survive tensions, problems, and all the things that are a part of our daily lives in these hectic times.

Relatives Who Live In

Parents or other adult relatives who live in the home can be either a delightful or a dreadful experience, depending upon the attitudes of those involved. Married children must realize that these relatives need to be treated with dignity. They are not to be treated as adopted children or as permanent baby-sitters. Parents who live in must remember that the home belongs to the children. They are not to function as managers of the home, but as guests. They must allow their married children the freedom to rear their own children in accordance with their own values. They must allow their married children the freedom to mature and succeed through their own mistakes and decisions. The "leaving" aspect of marriage can and should be a reality, even though the parents may live under the same roof. Attitudes, not locations, make the difference.

The situation can be a happy one if the adults remember they are adults and live with Christ's Spirit within. A healthy attitude is to think of the situation as one family living together, rather than two families existing together. The parents should have the freedom to make suggestions without the fear of intruding. The married children should have the liberty to include the parents in family plans without feeling burdened. The answer to any possible tension lies in adequate communication, with reciprocal respect and love.

Children

The Bible teaches that children are blessings to a family; however, we should not conclude that a childless couple is denied God's blessing. The interpersonal relationships between the parents and children help the parents to accept and live with their respective roles. These relationships also condition the developmental process of the children. (Read Deuteronomy 7:13; Psalms 127:4, 5; 128:3, 4; Proverbs 10:1; 15:20; 17:6; 23:13-15.)

Many people are too quick to blame parents for the conduct of children. Although parents do share the responsibility for the lifestyle of their children, we must not forget that peer groups wield great power in molding children's attitudes. God commands children to obey their parents, probably one reason is because of the outside pressures on them.

These varied magnetic pulls outside the home will inject disunity into the home, if they are heeded. Children are responsible to reject such pulls by adhering to their parents with honor and obedience. Children are to reject whatever goes against the teaching of their godly parents (gist of the entire book of Proverbs). Read Proverbs 1:8-16. "Hear, my son, your father's instruction, and do not forsake your mother's teaching" (v. 8).

During Old Testament times, failure on the part of the children to heed their father's instruction was considered such a serious threat to the stability of the home and society that rebellious children were stoned to death (Deuteronomy 21:18-21). This sounds harsh, but outright rebellion that is not curbed can pass from one generation to another (Jeremiah 28:16; 29:32), until a whole nation becomes rebellious (Isaiah 30:9; Ezekiel 2:3; 3:26, 27). We can see such results in our own nation after an era of permissive behavior.

Children should be taught to obey their parents. Then they will be better prepared to face the powerful outside influences when they are old enough to be away from home. Children who make autonomous decisions must share the blame for a chaotic society.

Husband and Wife Before and After Sin

Let us compare the relationship of the first husband and wife before they decided to sin with their relationship after they sinned. Many people feel that the relationship of the man and woman changed after their sin.

56

Adam and Eve's decision to sin was made before they had experienced any sin. They first sinned in the created state that God had declared was "very good" (Genesis 1:31). In that state they had the ability to choose evil as well as good. Man's desire for autonomy and independence did not begin after the "fall," but before it. Otherwise, Satan would have had no one to tempt.

What was the woman's place before sin? The woman was a helper fit for the man. She was equal in dignity, created out of the same stuff as man. The two became one flesh. They were naked, but they were not ashamed. God never created the body as an evil prison house for the soul. The physical body is included in God's declaration of "very good." What was woman's place after sin? She was still a helper fit for the man. Sin did not diminish that status. Because she is needed as man's complement, the Old Testament honors her role: "Rejoice in the wife of your youth" (Proverbs 5:18); "He who finds a wife finds a good thing, and obtains favor from the Lord" (18:22); "A prudent wife is from the Lord" (19:14); "Her worth is far above jewels" (31:10).

Is the woman still equal in dignity? Yes! Are the husband and wife still considered a unit after the "fall"? Yes! Jesus always referred to the unit when asked about marriage. He never suggested that it was broken by sin. Do not miss the significance of this! We cannot permit male arrogance to continue. Arrogance is sin, no matter who expresses it. Because woman is from man (Genesis 2:21-25), she becomes united with him in marriage (Genesis 2:24). The way a husband treats his wife is the way he treats himself (Ephesians 5:28). Competition was not to replace complementation after the fall into sin. Neither mate should try to exploit the other.

Were they still naked and not ashamed after the "fall"? No (Genesis 3:7, 10). Why? It certainly was not because their bodies were evil. God created physical bodies with the obvious sexual differences. Was it because they had not engaged in sexual intercourse before sin? Probably not. Sexual intercourse is not sin between married partners. To be naked is to be completely honest, with nothing hidden. Hiding is an act of deception, not of being honest or open. Humans are psychosomatically whole persons. When we have a reason to hide one aspect of our lives, we will often express that form of deception in other aspects also. I suspect that is what happened in the Garden of Eden. Before the fall, Adam and Eve had nothing to hide from each other or from God, so they did not deceive in any way. They were not ashamed of what they saw in each other. They were a unit. Adam was Eve's head even before the fall. As a unit they were to proceed in harmony toward life's goals. (It is possible that Eve began to hide some of her thoughts from Adam. She wanted to partake of the one tree that was forbidden, but she was not open with her husband about it. She did not share her desires with her husband. This could have been the action that created the weak spot which gave Satan leverage.)

Anytime one begins to harbor thoughts that are out of harmony with the mutual goals of the unit, he needs to share those thoughts with his mate. The direction and protection can be provided by the other. This is the interpersonal communication and confession husbands and wives need. But when one begins to harbor thoughts as a private matter, those thoughts can cut into the cleaving relationship of husband and wife. Satan will entice with those secret thoughts. Such enticements are calculated to draw the attention and commitment of one away from the other. Then the relationship between the two is no longer open and honest. When this happens, they can no longer stand to be naked. A cover-up takes place, and it may be expressed in either or both of two dimensions. The first is physical. One may not want to be seen naked by the other. We would probably be surprised how often this happens in marriage. There is not a complete openness between the two when this occurs. But this is not to condone or encourage the thoughts of some contemporaries who say we should have universal nakedness to foster universal honesty. Genesis 2 and 3 concern only a husband and wife. Later, after the fall, God provided clothing (3:21) and intended some clothing to be worn. However, He does expect a husband and wife to be naked in one another's presence without being ashamed.

The second dimension is a psychological cover-up. The tendency is for one to put on a psychological mask. Adam and Eve also experienced this dimension, for neither admitted his own desires. Instead, they both avoided personal responsibility for sin by placing the blame elsewhere (3:12, 13). Blaming others is a way of self-protection, a way of putting on a mask so others will not see us as we really are. Adam and Eve were no longer living for the other's perfection, but for their own protection. Each had erred, but neither wanted to be known as having made a mistake. Each tried to cover up physically and psychologically.

If there is any *one* thing husbands and wives need to work out from the beginning of the marriage, it is to overcome the attitude of independence. Eve's initial mistake was in her act of individualism and independence from her husband. Then she sinned against God who ordained the unit of husband and wife. If each had functioned properly as part of the unit, drawing guidance, strength, and protection from the other, neither would have sinned. Harboring secret desires, hopes, and dreams serves to weaken the unit. Secretiveness unglues the cleaving relationship. Both positive and negative ideas and desires should be shared, discussed, and handled together.

Because husbands and wives live much of their day in separate environmental pressures, it is common for one mate to begin to harbor dreams and desires that the other does not have. The husband may associate with people who live with material goals and symbols. The wife may have dreams based on afternoon television serials that the husband never sees. Because of the diversity of daily activities, the husband and wife should keep their communication with each other open and grounded to their mutual goals.

Was the woman cursed to a position after the fall that was inferior to her position before the fall? No! Some believe that the fall took all rights away from the woman, and she was cursed to the role of submission to her husband. In the Genesis account, the wife's role with the husband and children did not change after the fall.

Let us examine the passage that is usually considered (Genesis 3:16). *(I have alphabetized the thoughts in this verse so that it will be easier to refer to them in the discussion that follows.)* "To the woman He said, (a) 'I will greatly multiply your pain in childbirth.' " The literal translation of this is, "By multiplying, I will multiply your sorrow indeed your pregnancy." Why did God do this? I doubt that it was because God was angry and was repaying "evil for evil." The multiplication in bodily sorrow was due probably to the imbalance in nature caused by man's separating from God. It is clear that man's sin brought disharmony into nature (Romans 8:19-23). Peace within nature is dependent upon man's being at peace with God. It is God's intention to restore harmonious relationships by reuniting all things, man and nature, in Christ (Ephesians 1:9, 10; Colossians 1:19, 20).

God's words to Adam and Eve were not curses, but announcements about the consequences caused by the imbalance in nature. Man's sin brought imbalance to God's created ecology. Eve's sin

59

did not initiate pain in pregnancy and childbirth, but multiplied it. Now there would be a potential threat to the life of the mother. Pain, *per se,* is not evil. It is good. It is God's design for our protection, to alert us to danger. Nothing in Genesis suggests that Adam and Eve experienced no pain before the fall. If they had stubbed their toes on a rock, they would have felt pain. Pain is one of God's built-in protective devices. After the fall, nature posed a threat to life itself. Even the life-*producing* situation (pregnancy and childbirth) could now be a life-*taking* situation.

God would not permit the sorrow surrounding pregnancy to be so severe that the woman would not desire children. Jesus indicated the limited effect of this pain when He said, "Whenever a woman is in travail she has sorrow, because her hour has come; but when she gives birth to the child, she remembers the anguish no more, for joy that a child has been born into the world" (John 16:21). Producing life will overshadow the presence of pain.

God promised that the presence of pain would not be so great that the woman would not desire further sexual intercourse with her husband. This is seen in statement (b): "Yet your desire shall be for your husband." The promise assured that the multiplication of pain in pregnancy and childbirth would not cut into the physical cleaving relationship of the husband and wife.

God further promised that the pain would not be so harsh that the woman would seek to live apart from the man. If the pain turned the woman against sexual intercourse, it would lead to alienation from her husband. If that happened, she would not have her needs met as a person. God affirmed that this built-in result of sin would not interfere with the husband and wife roles. Statement (c), "And he shall rule over you," was part of God's promise, which was introduced by the word "yet" in (b). This word affirmed that both sexual desire and the rule of the husband were present before the fall, and it affirmed that both would continue afterward. The sin of Adam and Eve did not disrupt the family unit or change the family roles.

Eve's place of submission was not given to her as part of God's curse (which He never gave), but as a part of God's creation. Adam was the head of the wife from the beginning. Part of Eve's sin was that she acted independently of her head in obeying the lure of the serpent. In that instance she acted as a self-appointed authority. Paul referred to this incident as a basis for refusing to let the woman teach or have authority over the man (1 Timothy 2:12-14). Some say that Paul was referring to the curse of the woman, but this is not so. He was referring to God's order of creation (v. 13). Why is it that a woman should not have authority over man? It disrupts the family order of God. Women's oppression over men was stated as one reason for the degeneration of Israel (Isaiah 3:12).

For Eve's own fulfillment and protection, not her inferiority, God promised that the man would continue to keep his place as head of the unit. (We shall consider more specifically, in another chapter, the roles of the partners, to see their value for individual growth and family harmony.)

For Consideration or Discussion

1. For group discussion:
   What is the role of a husband in a Christian family? Of a wife? Of a child? Of a parent? Of a grandparent?
   Are the parenting roles of father and mother different? If so, in what way?
   Are these roles fixed or interchangeable?
   How can a single parent make up for the role of the missing spouse?
2. For private meditation:
   Who was dominant in your family, your father or mother?
   Has that affected the way you relate to your spouse? If so, how?

He's the Head

7

"For the husband is the head of the wife" (Ephesians 5:23).

This verse is threatening to many wives, but it doesn't have to be. Headship does not carry with it the negative connotations that the secular chain-of-command model often gives it.

Headship Does Not Mean Superiority

From the creation, male and female were to share dignity. Both were created in the image of God. Although male and female are physically and functionally different, they are not different in status.

Man is no more superior to woman because he is her head than God is superior to Jesus because He is Jesus' head. The New Testament teaches that God is Christ's head (1 Corinthians 11:3), but it also affirms their essential equality (John 1:1; 10:30; Philippians 2:6; 1 John 5:20). As God and Jesus do not have a superior/inferior relationship, neither should a husband and his wife.

The "chain of command" for the family should not be drawn as a vertical chart with man at the top, followed by wife and children. In our culture that communicates condescension. The picture is more like a circular chart with God in the center, and the family members rotating around Him. The circular chart affirms that man is the head, but also it recognizes that each person has a need for the other and complements the other. No one is "put down."

On any vertical chart, the place for the man is at the bottom, since headship comes from serving all (Matthew 20:25-28). This place would communicate service and support (bottom to top), not dictatorship (top to bottom).

Headship Does Not Mean Intelligence

To say that the husband is the head does not say that he is the smarter. It's easy to see how some might think that way though. "Where are all the brains in a body? In the head, right? So, shut up, stupid! I'm the head!"

But headship says nothing about IQ. I do not know what my wife's IQ is, and I do not want to find out. She was the first person in the history of her alma mater to graduate with a straight A average. I graduated the year after her, but I did not become the second person in the history of the college to graduate with that average.

A circuit judge who is a friend illustrated this principle of headship well. "While I am in the courtroom I am the 'head' in the relationship there. I am not the head because I am superior to anyone or smarter than anyone. But it is my responsibility that allows peace and order to exist. As I leave the courtroom, often school is letting out. When I come to a school crossing, a twelve-year-old safety patrol stands with his hand up. He is the 'head' of that crossing. That doesn't mean he is superior to me or smarter than I. He is simply carrying out a responsibility. Without such 'heads,' chaos results in any relationship."

Headship Does Not Mean Dictatorship

Being the head of the family does not mean that the husband is to function as a drill sergeant or four-star general. It doesn't carry through with the attitude we learned in the military: "It's not for you to reason why. It's just for you to do or die."

The family relationship is to be one of fellowship, *koinonia*-style. It is a common oneness that has a common mindedness. Headship does not mean that the husband makes all the decisions autocratically while the wife simply bows down. Jesus balanced that potential view when He described husbands and wives as being yoked together. By using the work "yoke," Jesus spotlighted the teamwork that should exist in the husband/wife relationship. Each member of the team is needed within a mutually submissive relationship. That's partly because each is different, and each has something to contribute to the team in a reciprocal way. God wants the husband and wife to make decisions in concert or in concord with each other. The wife has some abilities that the husband does not have. There are areas in which women are more knowledge-able than men. It would be in opposition to God's creation of woman if husbands did not appreciate their wives' abilities or disregarded them. It would be in opposition to God who gave women minds if they were not allowed to help make decisions.

The husband's decisions must not thwart the charisma God has given the wife. They must not prevent her from being a complement to him and he to her. The Bible affirms that a woman opens her mouth with wisdom (Proverbs 31:26), and a man should incline his ear to the words of the wise (Proverbs 1-8; 6:20-23; 22:17).

Headship Does Not Mean Origin or Source

While the Greek word for "head" does mean origin or source in some places (such as the head of a river), it is not accurate to suggest that it means that in every context. The Greek word used here for "head" also refers to someone with a kind of authority, although not necessarily dictatorial. Ephesians 1 says that Jesus is "head over all things to the church" (1:22). This verse does not mean merely source. Jesus' headship is also lordship.

Headship Does Not Mean Patronizing

The wife is not to be treated as an inadequate child. As Christ has confidence in the church, His bride, so should the husband have confidence in his bride.

Christ delegated authority and responsibility to the church, but Christ, the head, and the church function as a united team. The same kind of team relationship we see in the Godhead, even though the Father is recognized as head.

God, Jesus, and the Holy Spirit can all be referred to as Creator in the Bible. Both God and Jesus are called Savior. All three are called sources of peace. They are so involved in each other that what one does is often identified with the other two.

In the same way, husband and wife must work as a team with mutual consent that the husband is the captain of the team. A family without a functioning head is in as much trouble as a physical body without a functioning head. Again, this does not mean that the head is superior, for all parts are needed. (See 1 Corinthians 12:1ff.) But a family with two heads is as much of a freak as a body with two heads.

Headship Means Servant/Leadership

What is leadership? Leadership is influence. To the degree a person influences another, he is a leader. If you want to check out whether or not you are a leader, look to see if anyone is following. However, just because people follow is not enough to monitor. The more important question to ask is, "Why is someone following?" It may be because the "leader" carries a big stick or yells loud threats.

The better a person serves the needs of others, Biblically, the greater is his leadership. Jesus said,

> "You know that the rulers of the Gentiles lord it over them, and their great men exercise authority over them. It is not so among you, but whoever wishes to become great among you shall be your servant, and whoever wishes to be first among you shall be your slave; just as the Son of Man did not come to be served, but to serve, and to give His life a ransom for many" (Matthew 20:25-28).

So leadership comes in the package of servanthood.

Although it does not mean autocratic decision making, someone has to make final decisions when there is no concensus. There are times when husbands and wives do not agree on a decision. Ever have that happen in your marriage? When this happens, the husband must assume the leadership and make the decision—even if he goofs.

Headship Means Loveship

After Paul wrote, "For the husband is the head of the wife," he wrote, "Husbands, love your wives, just as Christ also loved the church and gave Himself up for her" (Ephesians 5:25).

A man might say, "But Jesus doesn't have *my* wife." However, Christ loves the church no matter what weaknesses and imperfections show up. The Greek word for love here *(agape)* refers to the unconditional commitment to an imperfect person.

The husband has the responsibility to set the love tempo for the whole family. If his temperament is wrong, his wife's needs will not be fully met, and the children will be deficient as well. When the husband loves his wife as Christ loves the church, he will discover that love comes back to him. He will receive what he gives. That's why Paul wrote, "He who loves his own life loves himself." To love your *wife* is to love your *life*.

Headship Involves Humbly Helping the Wife

Christ did not hesitate to give himself. He did it in such humble ways as attending a wedding despite a busy schedule (John 2), missing meals (John 4), touching the despised sick (John 5), and giving up periods of rest (John 6:15-20). He did not retaliate when murmured against (John 7). He took the brunt of criticism, even though He was right (John 9). Jesus wept in front of a crowd (John 11), washed the feet of His disciples (John 13), and withstood mistreatment without rebuke (John 18:1—19:11). He died voluntarily so others could live (John 19:17, 18). This describes the kind of self-giving love that the husband is to have for the wife (Ephesians 5:25).

Our teaching is backwards when we suggest that the home is the man's castle to dominate as the king. The home is not the husband's one-woman harem to provide him with comforts and protect him from displeasure. The following scene is all too common today: The husband moves from the dinner table to occupy his television chair for the remainder of the evening. The wife does the dishes, plays a bit with the children, helps with their homework, reads to them, helps them with their baths and preparations for bed, picks up their toys, and falls into bed literally exhausted. Then the husband cannot understand why she is too tired for sex. He has been excited through television programs, but she has been exhausted from tedious chores. Her lack of response may not indicate her lack of rapture late in the day so much as her lack of respect earlier in the day.

Peter spoke about the kind of consideration the husband should have for his wife: "You husbands likewise, live with your wives in an understanding way, as with a weaker vessel, since she is a woman; and grant her honor as a fellow-heir of the grace of life, so that your prayers may not be hindered" (1 Peter 3:7). The words "grant her honor" mean to show respect. The effectiveness of a Christian man's prayers depends partly upon his fulfillment of his responsibility as head of the household.

Some husbands will say, "I'm the head of the house!" Oh? Then you should read Philippians 2:3-7. "Do nothing from selfishness or empty conceit, but with humility of mind let each of you regard one another as more important than himself; do not merely look out for your own personal interests, but also for the interests of others. Have this attitude in yourselves which was also in Christ Jesus, who, although He existed in the form of God, did not regard equality with God a thing to be grasped, but emptied Himself, taking the form of a bondservant." Jesus demonstrated what it meant to be a man par excellence, and He was exalted through His humility (vv. 8, 9).

Headship Means Putting Self-Interests Second

Neither the job, desire for advancement or prestige, leisure, hobby, the dog, entertainment, nor sports should be allowed to come between the cleaving relationship with the wife. The husband must put his wife's well-being ahead of his own interests, just as Christ puts our well-being first. Would you want Christ to value an automobile, sports, or the lodge above you? Remember, your bride is to be loved as Christ loves His bride, the church. You should put her interests and well-being above yourself. Christ has given you the example.

Headship Involves Protection and Care for the Wife

Christ gave himself up for His bride, for her spiritual well-being (Ephesians 5:25). The husband must be the spiritual leader. How shameful it would be for a husband to lead his wife to Hell! The husband who is not a spiritual leader is not a man patterned after Christ.

Being the spiritual leader involves both attitudes and activities, inside and outside the scheduled gatherings of the saints. The Bible teaches that the responsible spiritual leadership of the husband is more concerned with his activities and attitudes with his wife than with his activities and attitudes in the church meetings. For instance, effective prayers in the home depend upon the husband's gentlemanly attitude about his wife (1 Peter 3:7). Effective protection against the wife's yielding to sexual temptations depends upon the husband's fulfilling his duty to his wife sexually (1 Corinthians 7:3). The stability of the family depends upon the husband's manifesting the attitudes of a spiritual leader at home (1 Timothy 3:2-5). Certainly involvement in church meetings is not to be neglected, but it cannot replace a man's responsibility at home.

Headship Involves Affectionate Care

A husband is not only to love his wife as Christ loves the church, but he is to nourish and cherish her as he does his own body (Ephesians 5:28, 29). As the church is now the body of Christ, the woman is a part of the man. Whatever a man does to the church, he does to Christ, and whatever he does to his wife, he does to himself.

"Nourish" and "cherish" were words once used to describe a nurse's motherly and tender care for a child. As a child needs more than mere physical necessities, so does the wife. A healthy child needs a soft hand and sweet talk, and so does the wife. She thrives on the handholding and "I love yous" far more than the man does. Maybe the married man gets a little thrill out of these, but he is made differently. The woman needs such tender expressions of the man's love.

Too often we have turned around whose initial responsibility it is to nourish and cherish. Many men act like boys wanting "mother" to feed them, so they can go and play their games and then be comforted when they get hurt. Biblically, the husband has that initial role. Have you ever noticed how little girls need Daddy's lap and his hugs? These little girls are mothers-in-the-making. When they become mothers, they still need such affectionate attention. When they receive it, they will respond with nourishing and cherishing of the husband, not out of duty but out of delight.

Someone may ask, "What if the wife doesn't respond with the kind of love the husband gives? What if she continues to nag, nettle, and nip?" Here again the husband has the responsibility to love as Christ loves. He loves regardless of the response. His love is steadfast. Christ's love for the church is not altered by the church's negative response. Neither should the husband's love be altered by the wife's negative reaction. He has the responsibility to continuously initiate love, whatever the circumstances. This is a tall order, but it is what it means to love the bride as Christ loves His bride.

The price may be high, but the dividends are fantastic. Unloveliness can change to loveliness. As Christ's kindness is the power to change the church (Romans 2:4), so the husband can change his wife. Indeed, he has the responsibility to so love her that he may present her to God as changed, sanctified, cleansed, and holy. It is in the context of making this point that Paul wrote, "For this cause a man shall leave his father and mother, and shall cleave to his wife;

and the two shall become one flesh" (Ephesians 5:31). May each husband love his wife as himself, for she is a part of him.

For the sake of order, God has established headship in the family. Any organization needs a head, which is not to say that the one appointed is necessarily the most intelligent. A vice-president of a company may be more brilliant than the president, and he must be in some areas in order to be a good complement. The two should not compete for decision-making successes, but cooperate in mutual trust and confidence. They need to share each other's abilities, resources, and experiences. When a decision cannot be made by mutual consent, the vice-president must concede to the president's decision and abide by it. This system works the same way in the family.

The husband must trust his wife and make her feel comfortable making decisions. Just as the church has many rights (order of worship, time, frequency of meetings), so does the wife. Her rights are all under the umbrella of living in unity with her husband. When the husband functions as a loving head without wishy-washy attitudes, he meets the wife's need to depend upon someone. She can trust him as she leans upon him, because he is living out the male role as God intended. She is actually freer to function with her God-given nature. With a husband who functions as he should, she does not have to drain her energies trying to think and live like a technological man. If the husband is a loving head, the wife is free to express her basic nature of sympathy, care, kindness, tenderness, and nurture to him. If the husband thwarts her expression of these qualities at home by forcing her to live like a man, her femininity will be imprisoned.

As the husband must be the head of the wife, so Christ must be the head of the husband. The husband must respond to Christ's headship in such a way that his decisions will be Christ's. The husband has no right to live in competition with his Head in making decisions. Neither should the wife live in competition with her husband.

Peter sums up the husband's relationship with his wife with a classic statement. "You husbands likewise, live with your wives in an understanding way, as with a weaker vessel, since she is a woman; and grant her honor as a fellow-heir of the grace of life, so that your prayers may not be hindered" (1 Peter 3:7). *Man, are you giving her understanding, tenderness, and honor? If you aren't, why aren't you?*

69

For Consideration or Discussion

1. For husbands only:
   Has this chapter caused you to re-think your understanding of the phrase, "The husband is the head of the wife"? If so, are you willing to share those thoughts with the group?
   Check yourself. I exercise my headship by:
   Taking my place at the bottom, serving the family. Yes_____ No_____ Sometimes_____
   By recognizing and encouraging my wife's abilities. Yes_____ No_____ Sometimes_____
   By trying to create a climate for good fellowship in the family. Yes_____ No_____ Sometimes_____
   Consulting my wife on all major decisions. Yes_____ No_____ Sometimes_____
   My willingness to help my wife with household chores, getting up in the night to care for a child, sharing in changing diapers, etc. Yes_____ No_____ Sometimes_____
   My willingness to take responsibility for major decisions when a consensus is not possible. Yes_____ No_____ Sometimes_____
2. For wives only:
   Are you willing to acknowledge your husband's headship by:
   Deferring to him on major decisions when a consensus does not seem possible? Yes_____ No_____ Sometimes_____
   When the decision is made, supporting your husband even though you do not agree completely? Yes_____ No_____ Sometimes_____
   Using your own gifts and carrying your share of the responsibilities, so that "headship" does not become an intolerable burden to him? Yes_____ No_____ Sometimes_____

The Woman
of the House

8

Are you mad, sad, or glad you are a woman?

Some women who are mad or sad because they were born female are blaming God. But God can't be blamed. In fact, it is easier to make a case that God put women on a pedestal when He created them. After God looked at the world He had created, He said, "It was good." But when He created the male, He said, "It is *not* good" (Genesis 2:18). It was only after the woman was on earth that God saw, "It was *very* good" (Genesis 1:31).

When God created man, He called him by the Hebrew word "ish." The Hebrew word for woman is "ishah." (I suspect God looked at man and said "ish," but looked at woman said "ish . . . *ah*.")

God has always used women to help turn around significant trends in history. When God's people were on the verge of being annihilated, because the Pharaoh had sent out an order that all the baby boys should be murdered at birth, do you know who saved the day? Some courageous women (midwives) who disobeyed Pharaoh's order. At another time, God's people were in a period of history where they were going up and down like yo-yos. When they got down into the pits, they would cry out for a deliverer. One of the deliverers that God chose became their religious and the civic and the military leader. The leader was a woman—Deborah. At another time, an order had been given by the king, due to the influence of one of his cohorts, that all the Jews should be murdered. A woman saved the day by appealing to the king—Esther.

Between the Old and New Testament periods, there was another time when God's people were on the verge of being annihilated. One of the pagan rulers, Antiochus IV, decided the way to eliminate

71

God's people was to eliminate their religion. So he learned what God commanded the people to do, and he sent out a federal order: "You *cannot* do it." He also looked at what God commanded His people not to do, and he sent out a federal order: "You *must* do this."

One of the things he discovered was, God's people were to circumcise their baby boys on the eighth day. He sent officers to the Jewish communities to insure that they didn't do it. We read in history that two women in one community had their boys circumcised despite the command. When the officers discovered what they had done, they took the infant sons, tied ropes around their necks, and tied the other ends of the ropes around the breasts of the mothers. They made the mothers stand and watch their infant sons strangle to death. Then they paraded the mothers, with their sons hanging from them, down the streets of the village. Would you be willing to obey God if you knew something like that would happen to you?

During that same period of time, some officers came into a village and ordered the people to eat pork. In the village was a widow who had seven sons. The sons were lined up, and the officers said, "Okay, boys, put the pork into your mouths." Boy number one refused to do it. They scalped the boy, cut out his tongue, and cut off his hands and his feet. Then they heated some big pans and fried the boy. They did that to son number two, son number three, and son number four. You just can't help but ask, "How did those boys get the courage to refuse?"

They did it to son number five, and to son number six. With just one son left, the officer began to weaken, and he felt sorry for the mother. He went to the mother and begged her, by saying, "Mother, please just talk to this last son of yours, and ask him to put the pork into his mouth."

The historian who was there said that after much persuasion the mother agreed to talk to her son. She said, "Son, for nine months I carried you in my womb, and for nearly three years I nursed you. I got up in the wee, early hours of the morning when you were sick and cared for you. I have brought you to this point in your life. Now, this afternoon, I have seen all of my other sons killed. So I beg you, Son, please, please, out of respect to me your mother, and what I've done for you, do not fear that butcher's knife. Be willing to die a death worthy of the God who gave you to me. The same God who gave you to me once will give you to me again."

72

When they came to the boy, he put out his arms and his tongue and said, "Take them." God has used women.

But we are living in a time when many women feel that it is dumb, and boring, and frustrating, and wrong to give themselves to being wives and mothers. My wife, who is a college graduate, would say the opposite. She would say it is not boring and frustrating. If she had to go and work somewhere eight hours a day, and do the same thing day in and day out, that would be restrictive to her. She says that being a wife and a mother is the most freeing, the most nonrestrictive, and the most expanding thing she can do.

For instance, she can move in and out of a lot of different things during the course of a day. Women need to be reminded of this. She can be an "Emergency 51" and a rampart all at the same time. She can be a kindergarten teacher, and a fourth-grade teacher, and an eighth-grade teacher, and a ninth-grade teacher, and nobody's checking up on her credentials. She can be an RN, and a medical doctor, and nobody's worrying about her degrees. She can also be a judge, and a jury, and a prosecuting attorney, and an executioner within four minutes. She can be a fashion designer, or she can be an interior decorator.

Isn't it odd that we're living in a day when so many people do not want children? Yet people are the only kind of life made in the image of God.

We need to take more seriously the significant roles of wives and mothers. I think one of our problems, is that we've gone for the wrong role model.

Women, be careful about the role models that you choose. Being a housewife and a mother does not have to be frustrating and dumb and boring. Joseph Cardinal Mindzenty once wrote,

> The most important person on earth is a mother. She cannot claim the honor of having built Notre Dame Cathedral. She need not. She has built something more magnificent than any cathedral—a dwelling place for an immortal soul, the tiny perfection, her baby's body. The angels have not been blessed with such a grace. They cannot share in God's creative miracle to bring new saints to Heaven. Only human mothers can. Mothers are closer to God, the Creator, than any other creature. What on God's good earth is more glorious than—TO BE A MOTHER.

Several years ago I meditated upon the value of my own mother. That caused me to write a mini-autobiographical sketch that showed her input into my life. The sketch is really a salute to mothers everywhere:

Who was the first to know that I was going to visit planet earth? You, Mom. And you announced it with joy, not disappointment.

Who was my first hostess, allowing me to live inside the home of her body? You, Mom. And you invited me to stay on and on—for nine months.

Who was the first to rearrange both herself and her schedule just because I was important? You, Mom.

Who was the first to show me the tenderness of a kiss? You, Mom.

Who was the first to introduce me to the beautiful sounds of a song? You, Mom.

Who was the first to offer me food when I was hungry? You, Mom.

Who was the first one to awake when I was restless in the middle of the night? You, Mom.

Who was the first to hold my body when it was feverish. You, Mom.

Who was the first to put a spoon in my hand and encourage me to do some things for myself? You, Mom.

Who was the first to pick me up when I fell? You, Mom.

Who was the first to care enough for me to discipline me? You, Mom.

Who was there waiting for me when I came home that first day of school? You, Mom.

Who was my fortress of peace and protection when I got scared? You, Mom.

Who was the first to say, "My, you look handsome, Son"? You, Mom.

Who was the one who said "Twinkle, Twinkle, Little Star," sounded great on the cornet? You, Mom.

Who understood when I experienced my first love sickness, and later heartbreak? You, Mom.

Who waited up for me to come in at night? You, Mom.

Who said, "We'll make it, Kids" when Dad died? (We were entering high school.) You, Mom.

Who was at the train station with tears on her cheeks as I left for military service? You, Mom.

Who wrote me that first letter in boot camp? You, Mom.

Who regularly slipped a dollar or two in her letters? You, Mom.

Who wrote to me twice a week when I was in Korea? You, Mom.

Who always subscribed to the home paper for me? You, Mom.

Who secretly paid off my car for me when I started college? You, Mom.

Who came to help out when I had pneumonia for ten days while my wife and I were in college? You, Mom.

Who was the first to hold my first child? You, Mom.

Who was the first to take a picture of that child in the hospital? You, Mom.

It is no wonder that . . .

> There is a Jewish proverb saying, "God could not be everywhere and therefore he made mothers." Or a Spanish proverb saying, "An ounce of mother is worth a pound of clergy."

God's intention in making the woman was that she would contribute to the man's life with her uniqueness: one life created by God united with another life created by God. Each woman has her own individuality, her own charisma. To submit to her husband in the highest sense is not to bypass that uniqueness, or to suppress it. To submit will allow it to develop so that what the woman is as a person will be shared with her husband. God wants expressive or creative submission, not computerized submission. Each woman has a self to share.

We must never equate a submissive wife with a suppressed wife. Legalism will do that, but love will not. The husband is given the mandate to love his wife as Christ loved the church. Loving the church, Christ freed it to function according to its intended nature (Galatians 5:1).

In expressing her ideas, projects, abilities, and personality for the well-being of her husband, the wife must remember to pour her femininity into those expressions. Many women seem to object to being women. They try to think and act like men. Neither husband, home, nor society needs this. More important, the woman does not need it. When she does this, the balance of maleness and femaleness is lost; and something of the image of God is blurred. God's image is expressed through the combination of maleness and femaleness, not through either one alone. (See Genesis 1:27, 28; where "man" refers to both male and female.)

The husband must allow the wife to develop and express her potentialities as a person; and to see these as a complement to him rather than as competition or a threat. Our society is worsened when a woman's individuality is suppressed in her submission. We can only guess how much better our world could be if women's creativity were shared in many areas of life. We can no longer use the Bible as our reason for preventing half of humankind from participating in planning and decision making. The good woman in Proverbs 31:10-31 expressed her individuality, interests, and abilities in many ways. In this passage of Scripture is the grandest word portrait ever painted by a pen:

76

An excellent wife, who can find? (v. 10a).

They had some of our problems back then, also.

For her worth is far above jewels (v. 10b).

Does that sound like she's not worth much? We don't have many jewels in our house, so let me paraphrase this. "Her worth is far above a new Cadillac and gasoline at three cents a gallon for unleaded." She's worth a lot!

The heart of her husband trusts in her (v. 11a).

She is trustworthy. She's not spending all their money as soon as the husband gets out of sight. She doesn't buy six pairs of shoes and hide them in the closet for six months. Then when he asks if they are new, she doesn't say, "Why no! I've had these at least six months."

She is trustworthy. He has full confidence in her handling of the affairs that accompany managing a household. She can be trusted with the total bank account. How can this be? Because she and her husband are a unit. Neither person is free from the influence of the other when they are separated. To be "one flesh" means they are committed to the same goals and function as a team in achieving those goals. If the husband does not love his wife, and if the wife does not submit to her husband, this kind of trust cannot develop.

And he will have no lack of gain (v. 11b).

She is such an enterprising wife that she helps keep the financial picture positive.

She does him good and not evil all the days of her life (v. 12).

This is one of the finest descriptions of submission in the Bible. She is living for his welfare. No wonder he has confidence in her.

She looks for wool and flax, and works with her hands in delight (v. 13).

Her disposition for caring is expressed in providing for her family. She is industrious and enjoys it. How can she be delighted with such a life? Because her husband is not forcing her to act like a man by his failure to function in his own God-designed role.

She is like merchant ships; she brings her food from afar (v. 14).

Like ships that sail away to bring goods from afar, she will travel to bring home the bargains. Doesn't that sound like a woman today? She drives twenty miles to take in a sale.

She rises also while it is still night, and gives food to her household (v. 15a).

Nobody is getting out of her house without breakfast. Probably we would be shocked to know how many people leave home without eating a bite. Hundreds of thousands of school children start their classes hungry. What's in the stomach affects what's in the head!

But this wife starts getting things ready for breakfast before the sun comes up. (And those were the days before alarm clocks.) Why? Well, if she wanted biscuits she couldn't go to the "frig," get out a cylinder, twist it, and watch the biscuits fall out. She had to make them from scratch. If she wanted some eggs, she would go outside, raise the hen, and gather the eggs.

And portions to her maidens (v. 15b).

She would make a list of prescribed tasks for the maids to do. I can hear you now: "If I had maids, I would get up before dawn, make a list for the maids. and then hit the sack again." I'll bet every person reading this has maids; we do in our house. (Now be sure you read the rest of this before you say, "Well, if he's that rich, I'm not going to read another word.")

Life was interesting when I was growing up. We lived in town, but we had no plumbing. We had a well in the backyard. We didn't even have enough money for a pump or a pulley for the bucket— just an open well with a bucket and rope beside it. We drew water for everything. If we wanted hot water, we heated it on the wood cookstove in the kitchen. We did have central heat. It was a coal stove that was located in the dining room—in the center of that four-room house. We carried in buckets of coal all day. I never knew anyone ever woke up to a warm house. Stepping on that linoleum with bare feet was like stepping on ice.

Unless someone has tasted that kind of living, he doesn't know what fantastic "maids" a theromostat, hot-water heater, automatic oven, and automatic washer and dryer are. Nearly every household has many "maids." They don't talk back, either!

We are living during wonderful times. I do not think that God will ever allow the pressures of a culture on our shoulders to outrun the parents' potential availability to help their children. Our children need input from their parents, now perhaps more than ever in the history of this country.

When I was growing up, the way we got into trouble was by turning over someone's outhouse. If we really wanted to be mean, we waited until someone was inside it.

The "hoods" in our high school (every high school had some) were those super mean kids who had all sorts of gadgets attached to their cars. Every once in a while they would buy a six-pack, drive way out into the country, and drink it. That is Mickey Mouse stuff today. Teenagers laugh at that as a joke from ancient days.

Today our kids are facing a tough world. They are getting a lot hurled at them. They hear words in movies that I never heard until I was an adult. They have pills to pep them up, wind them down, and prevent pregnancy. They have abortion clinics and booze available for the asking. They have drugs to shoot, drink, eat, and sniff. They have pornography at a finger's tip.

Could it be possible that God has permitted us our modern conveniences (including no-iron clothing) to help free up time so mothers can have more positive and meaningful and needed associations with their children? She has more time than ever to be creative and to use her various abilities and interests in helpful interpersonal activities. She has more time to pour herself into the lives of her family and into the future of her community.

However, if we aren't careful, we can fill up that time with too many non-family activities. Then the children actually have less time with mother than during those "ancient days" when they often worked with her in time-killing chores.

She considers a field and buys it. (v. 16a).

Now she is dabbling in real estate. I can hear men yelling: "Where did she get all that money?" She has been saving it up *from her earnings.* She has been doing some creative enterprising with her skills (v. 24), and making a profit (v. 18). The idea that only the man can "bring home the bacon" is not Biblical (v. 24).

"She stretches out her hands to the distaff, and her hands grasp the spindle" (v. 19.) Why is she creative with her skills? For three reasons: (1) She helps the poor: "She extends her hand to the poor; and she stretches out her hands to the needy" (v. 20). I suspect our welfare systems in this country would be better off if the government got out of them and returned them to the neighborhoods. (2) For her household: "She is not afraid of the snow for her household, for all her household are clothed with scarlet" (v. 21). She's personally interested in the kind of cloth her family wears. (3) For herself: "She makes coverings for herself; her clothing is fine linen and purple" (v. 22). Fine linen and purple were the best a woman could wear in those days. (It's like wearing neat double knits today.) She knew how to look sharp.

Please, girls, don't be an unkempt old bag when your husband comes home from work. He's been in public all day where women have looked sharp. Their hair wasn't in curlers, their teeth were in, perfume was used, and they had pleasant breaths. So don't meet your husband at the end of each day looking as if a tornado had made a direct hit.

But, fellows, if you want to see her freshened up and looking nice, then notice her and compliment her. Give her some money to buy some new clothes. Allow her to spend some money at the beauty salon. Take her out on a date—at least every ten days. If you can't afford anything else, go window shopping—but do it. Women enjoy being out—to get away for awhile.

Her husband is known in the gates, when he sits among the elders of the land (v. 23).

The location where men did their civic and business responsibilities was "the gates." Here her husband was known as a successful man. Surely part of the reason was because of the kind of wife he had. He was free to function as a man because she was functioning as a woman. They were complementing each other.

She opens her mouth in wisdom, and the teaching of kindness is on her tongue (v. 26).

She is not the type who is seen but not heard. Her speech is not stupid or sarcastic. She is a well-balanced woman, secure in her role. She has dignity, and evidently she enjoys being a woman. She does not have to use her intellectual abilities to "lord" it over others. She combines wisdom and kindness.

She looks well to the ways of her household (v. 27).

She is not too "intelligent" for humdrum duties. Through the medium of household duties, her wisdom has the most opportunity to be expressed. Because she functions as a mature, well-balanced, and happy woman, her family blesses and praises her. She is accepted and loved. Her children have no desire to run away from her, and her husband has no reason to "cut her down." This is a picture of a happy, balanced family. The leaving of parents, the cleaving relationship, and the oneness are all evident.

This woman in Proverbs has reached the height of meaningfulness because she respects the Lord's will for her life (v. 30). This is her liberation. She is praised in the gates. Who is praising her there? Her own husband—the one person who means the most to her and to whom she means the most. He is her number-one fan! If more men would respect their wives and praise them, especially before others, more children would learn respect for womanhood. Children need to learn this. If fathers would teach respect for women by their own example, we would see fewer girls mistreated, fewer prostitutes, fewer unwed mothers, and fewer belittled wives. Of course, the wife must do her part to deserve praise.

If someone ever asks again, "An excellent wife, who can find?" may you respond, "Why my husband—and he already has—me!"

Peter described the *AAA wife* (1 Peter 3:1-6) under the following categories:
Her actions

> "In the same way, you wives, be submissive to your own husbands so that even if any of them are disobedient to the word, they may be won without a word by the behavior of their wives, as they observe your chaste and respectful behavior."

Here is a woman who really knows how to act well. You may say, "Well, she must have a fantastic husband." Nope! He's a pagan. He won't go to church with her. He won't adopt her Christian value systems. He's probably a pain in the neck to live with. So what does she do? Pack up her bags and head for mother? No! Try to convert him by rehearsing the preacher's sermons, leaving tracts in his lunch bucket, pinning Scriptures on the mirror he uses for shaving? No! She observes a chaste and respectful behavior. The Greek word "observe" means to pay close attention to something. She gets her messages across by the way she acts and reacts, not by the way she talks and talks back.
Her attractiveness

> "And let not your adornment be external only—braiding the hair, and wearing gold jewelry, and putting on dresses."

This verse is not saying "look like a mess." Some people have read this and concluded that a woman should not wear jewelry or have her hair done. If that's what this verse is saying, then a woman shouldn't wear any clothing either.

Elsewhere we read that an excellent wife, Biblically speaking, knows how to look nice (Proverbs 31:22). Look and smell nice when your husband comes home from work. Let the one who sees you the most see you the best. It isn't likely that his eyes will roam if he has someone to see at home—someone that he likes watching.

However, the AAA wife doesn't pour *all* of her womanness in the way she looks externally. There is more to meaningful relationships than living with a live "Barbie Doll" all day.

It gets very boring to just sit around and look at each other. Peter says to balance how you look externally to how you are internally. Tie the right kind of attitudes to your attractiveness. Then you will be beautiful inside out.

Her attitude

> "But let it be the hidden person of the heart, with the imperishable quality of a gentle and quiet spirit, which is precious in the sight of God. For in this way in the former times the holy women also, who hoped in God, used to adorn themselves, being submissive to their own husbands. Thus Sarah obeyed Abraham, calling him lord, and you have become her children if you do what is right without being frightened by any fear."

The AAA wife seeks to overhaul the "hidden person of the heart." A gentle and quiet spirit is a meek person, not a weak person. She has her temper under control. She doesn't fly off the handle or hit the ejection button when things start to fall apart. She is not easily disturbed, nor does she naturally disturb others when she is around. Tranquility and peace abound. What a beautiful household to live in. Since she isn't easily frightened, she doesn't terrify others.

I realize some days can really be the pits—especially when everything seems to be going wrong at home. Sandi Franklin has captured both the pits and the pleasures when she says:

> SOMEDAY, WHEN THE KIDS ARE GROWN, life will be different. The memo pad on my refrigerator will read, "Afternoon at hairdresser," or, "Browse through art gallery," or, "Start golf lessons," instead of, "Pediatrician at 2:00," or "Cub Pack Meeting."

> SOMEDAY, WHEN THE KIDS ARE GROWN, the house will be free of graffiti: There will be no crayoned smiley faces on walls, no names scrawled in furniture dust, no pictures fingered on steamy windows, and no initials etched in bars of soap.

82

SOMEDAY, WHEN THE KIDS ARE GROWN, I won't find brown apple cores under the beds, empty spindles on the toilet paper hanger, or fuzzy caterpillars in denim jeans. And I will be able to find a pencil in the desk drawer, a slice of leftover pie in the refrigerator, and the comics still in the center of the newspaper.

SOMEDAY, WHEN THE KIDS ARE GROWN, I'll breeze right past the gumball machine in the supermarket without having to inadvertantly pass the candy or toy sections; and I'll choose cereal without considering what noise it makes, what prize it contains, or what color it comes in.

SOMEDAY, WHEN THE KIDS ARE GROWN, I'll prepare Quiche Lorraine, or Scallops Amandine, or just plain liver and onions, and no one will say, "Yuk! I wish we were havin' hot dogs!" or "Jimmy's lucky—his mom lets him eat chocolate bars for dinner." And we'll eat by candlelight, with no one trying to roast their peas and carrots over the flame to "make them taste better," or arguing about who gets to blow out the candle when we're done.

SOMEDAY, WHEN THE KIDS ARE GROWN, I'll get ready for my bath without first having to remove a fleet of boats, two rubber alligators, and a soggy tennis ball from the tub. I'll luxuriate in hot, steamy water and billows of bubbles for a whole hour, and no fists will pound on the door—no small voices will yell, "Hurry up, Mommy. I gotta go!"

YES, SOMEDAY, WHEN THE KIDS ARE GROWN, life will be different. They'll leave our nest, and the house will be
   Quiet . . .
      and Calm . . .
         and Empty . . .
            and Lonely . . .
               And I won't like that at all.
And then I'll spend my time, not looking forward to Someday, but looking back at Yesterday.

Yes, some days can be the pits. But in the end, it is worth it all.

For Consideration or Discussion

1. Are you able to affirm the uniqueness of your female person-hood? Can you do that even though you are single? How?
2. Women, consider your uniqueness:
   You and you alone can bear children.
   You and you alone can nurse children.
   The softness of your body offsets the hardness of man.
   The gentleness of your personality softens a hard world.
   Your nurturing instincts provide the supportiveness required for human survival and growth.
   The Genesis account of your creation tells us that the world was lacking something until you entered it.
   You are not an addendum to the creation story, nor a postscript to it.
   You complete it and round it out.
   You and you alone can make a partial man a complete man.
   Within the uniqueness of your gender lies a portion of your uniqueness as a person. Have you discovered it yet? If not, search for it! Invite your closest friends to help you identify it. When you find it, affirm it, and celebrate it.

Single Parenting

9

Being single is not as unique as some might think. One hundred percent of the population have been single at one time, and most will be single again before death.

Single parenting is not new. It has always been around because of early deaths, wars, divorce, etc. In fact, the divorce rate in the fifties was higher than it is today.

However, partly because of a growing population, the number of single-parent families has doubled in the past ten years to 6.6 million families. One out of every five families with children has a single parent. One-half of all the children in this country will live in a single-parent home before he reaches his eighteenth birthday.

Most of the single-parent families are headed by a woman. Out of 6.6 million single-parent families, only 355,000 of them are headed by a man.

There are problems that automatically accompany many single-parenting situations. We will look at a few in this chapter.

The Emotional Stigmatism

Traditionally this has been a couple oriented society. However, forty percent of the adult population in the U.S. is single. For every three couples, there are four singles. All of us entered life a single. Most women will live out the last several years of their lives as singles. So being single is not *that* unusual.

However, the stigmatism is augmented when the single parent lives life worrying about what people think. Are they thinking *I* am the cause? Absolutely not! Most people do not try to figure out who is to blame for one parent being gone from a family. Don't stigmatize self and assume that it is the way everybody else sees you.

The stigmatism is also self-augmented when the single parent overreacts to a couple society. It is true that we have not given enough time and energy to helping the single parent. Most sermons in churches, articles about the family, and books deal more with two parents than the single parent. However, self-stigmatism can increase if you immediately tune out with the response, "That doesn't apply to me." Understand that many homes with two parents are having some serious problems, caused by two people trying to relate to each other and the children.

Two parents have problems the single parent does not have—competition, jealousy, envy, lack of trust, misunderstandings, incompatibility, infidelity, expectation gaps, etc. Having a partner in parenting isn't all that rosy. If it were, there would not be an increase in the number of single parents.

What are some ways to work through emotional stigmatism?
Develop some close friends.

Friendships have not received the priority they should in our culture. We have stressed independence too much. We tend to run away from what we need most—friends.

When you have been hurt in love, it is easy to give up all close relationships and make independence your new god. A person who does that turns whatever love he has left onto himself. But that will create more loneliness. It is a defense mechanism that hampers growth instead of helping it.

Don't just look for friends who give you all you think you need. No one person can do that. Seek out not only friends you need, but also some who need you. You can grow out of self-misery most rapidly when you reach out to touch someone else in need.

A real friend is someone you can be yourself with. Develop relationships in which you don't have to hide your feelings, your times of depression, your dreams, your inadequacies, etc. The more you pretend you are what you aren't, the more uncomfortable people may be in your presence. They may feel intimidated that you are so much better than they.

Single people can have an advantage in making friends. Married couples too often restrict their friendships to other married *couples*. That really reduces their friendship potentialities, because *four* people have to click in their friendship. Only eight percent of married people have a friend of the opposite sex.

Being single can multiply the resources of people who can touch your life and you theirs. Make friends with family units; with two parents as well as with individuals and other single-parent families. Your family needs the contribution that family units with two parents can give. Two-parent families need the contribution that single-parent families can provide. Every two-parent family unit ought to have some single-parent families as friends and vice versa. *Expand your family circle.*

"Adopt" others into your family relationships by having them over. Developing close friends will do this. But it is also important to expand your family circle by "adopting" some of the friends of your children. Let them be in your house. Include some of them in your family activities.

Find out what your family is good for, and make those things part of your family.

Children of a friend of mine, who has no partner listed several things a family is good for. Every one of them can be a part of a single-parent family. Here are some of them: (1) *A family is good for acceptance.* It's the place where people take you in even though you don't deserve it. A family doesn't have to have two parents for acceptance to happen. (2) *In a family learning takes place.* In a family we learn to do things, react, etc. (3) *A family is for traditions.* A single-parent family doesn't have to drop all traditions. Such things as the hanging of stockings at Christmas time, the hiding of baskets at Easter, the tooth fairy, etc. can be a part of any family. (4) *A family is for laughter.* (5) *A family is for fights.* (6) *A family is for doing things together.* (7) *A family is for talking and sharing.* (8) *A family is for discipline.*

Don't get mad at society because it is couple oriented.

Be thankful couples are still a part of our society. But don't sit around envying them. Sometimes having two parents isn't always that great for some families. Some people are married and have a mate around, but they are still "single parents."

Don't always blame the church and the people around you for not ministering to you more.

Some people honestly do not know what to say or do. They are afraid they will say or do something wrong.

Some singles just aren't very available or approachable. They are hard to help. Some carry a continual chip on their shoulders. Some have been hurt badly in their relationships and are still in pain. For them to think about the give and take needed in another caring relationship is like pouring salt in an open wound. Some singles have put themselves into such separated categories that if someone doesn't say "single parents" they think they are being ignored.

Recently I was one of two resource people at a family retreat. After my first talk, a woman came up to me and said, "That was fine, but you said nothing for me. I am a single parent." She had her children by her side. Can't you imagine the self-image and stigmatism she is reinforcing her kids to have about their family and themselves? She did the same thing to the second resource person. Many things were said for *people* regardless of their marital status, but this woman, who saw herself as totally distinct from others, would not see that.

Everybody has something distinct from others. Don't drown in your own distinctiveness. Allow yourself to swim in the universalities you share with other humans.

Watch your reactions.

Whether situations better or bitter your lot, depends a great deal upon the attitudes of the single parent. It is the parent's reaction more than other people's actions that sets the tone in the family.

None of us can control how other people act. We can influence them (sometimes), but we can't control them. However, we can control how we react. If we allow the actions of others to determine our reactions (and that is easy to do), we have voluntarily given the control of ourselves to others. When that happens, the single parent turns the reins of the family over to others, because our reactions set the temperament in the family.

Forgive your mate and yourself.

Few things can keep a person in despair more powerfully than holding grudges. Forgiveness frees us to appreciate today and anticipate what God has in store for tomorrow. "Let all bitterness and wrath and anger and clamor and slander be put away from you, along with all malice. And be kind to one another, tender-hearted, forgiving each other, just as God in Christ also has forgiven you" (Ephesians 4:31, 32).

Let go of fear.

The fear of failure in facing the future alone is one of the emotional stigmas that can accompany the divorced, single parent. It isn't just the loneliness that a person can fear. It is also the fear of failing again in any personal relationship. Two negative reactions can set in:

1. The single parent may crawl into a shell of isolationalism. This is the worst thing you can do. It means you are your own companion and friend. It can be pretty gloomy.

Get out. Other people need you—your personality, your laughter, your talents, etc. However, the single parent often doesn't think so. "After all, if the person who knows me best doesn't need me, then nobody does." Rubbish! Take your children to family-oriented events. Don't stay away from family retreats, church socials, etc., because families will be there. *Remember, you are a family! Act like one!*

2. The second reaction to the fear of failure is assimilation. You check in your own unique personality. You try to second guess what will please people, and then you try to conform to it. It comes from the fear of failure. But doing that cheats people from knowing you, and it robs you from being yourself. Kick fear out! Take charge of your personality and uniqueness which God created.

Dr. Gerald Jampolsky has written a book that every person should read. It is called *Love Is Letting Go of Fear.*

The past is past. Let go of it. A major step in letting go of fear is letting go of the past. Jampolsky lists some words we should eliminate: impossible, can't try, limitation, if only, but, however, difficult, ought to, should, doubt. Any words that place you or anyone else in a category, any words that lead to measuring or evaluating yourself or other people, any words that tend to judge or condemn should be eliminated.

Decide to change all thoughts that hurt self or others.

Decide not to let the past trap you into its negativism.

You can't change the past, but you can change yourself. I once read that a sign of depression is to decide unconsciously that it's safer to feel miserable and exhausted all the time than to change our lives.

To allow fear to have its day is to sin. Someone has described sin as:

S eparation
I ndependence
N egativism

Separation, independence, and negativism are three products of the fear of failure. We will separate from others; we will crawl inside the god of independence and look back at the world around us through the distorted lens of negativism.

Financial Anxiety

Most single-parent families are headed by women. Ninety per-cent of the working women in this country make less than $15,000 a year. Raising a family on that amount is super tough.

Alimony can be helpful. Don't feel like a beggar receiving alimony. If you have agreed to raise the children, you need help. Here are some suggestions:

1. *Be willing to work.* It can shatter the self-image of a woman to have to work who was raised to believe that only a man should be the breadwinner. She may feel like she is abandoning what she has prepared herself to do—be a wife and mother. However, being a working mother is not a new situation. I grew up during what some people call the "good-ole-days." Wholesome family life seemed to be a national trademark. But we had a factory in our little town of four thousand that hired women primarily. When WW II began, women in the U.S. drove trucks, built tanks, built buildings, etc. I have never lived in an age when women did not work.

Today only a small percentage of families in the U.S. have non-working mothers. Working mothers do not have to harm their chil-dren.

2. *Have someone give you financial counsel.* Don't spend money on the car or house with the first estimate you get. Ask others about little ways to save on purchasing, bank accounts, paying bills, etc.

3. *Be honest with the children about finances.* Sit down and explain the situation. Let them help you with the budget. It might help motivate them to turn out lights, shut doors, keep the thermo-stat down, restrict toll calls, etc.

4. *Let the children work.* Don't be so protective of them that you think they should not work. Most children need more of a sense of responsibility and fulfillment.

5. *Don't compensate for the lack of one parent.* Children do not need to participate in everything. Children with two parents want to do the same thing. You need to set limits and communicate the limits to them early.

Relationships Change

A single parent may experience many changes in relationships.
1. *The relationship with the former mate changes.* However,

maintaining a friendship with the "ex" is far preferable to being enemies.

2. *Relationship with the children can change.* After all, the children now have one-half parents they formerly had. No single parent can compensate for that by trying to be both parents. You are *one* parent and one parent only. The sooner a single parent understands and accepts this, the better off the family will be. If one parent tries too hard to be the *other* parent as well, the characteristics of the parent who lives with the children will get lost. Then the children will lose something valuable—the unique personality and aptitudes of that parent.

Children *do* need role models of the sex that is not living with them. But that can come only from someone who is that gender. It should come from other family members or close friends. A mother cannot be a role model of a man. And a man cannot be a role model of a woman.

Let your children be your partners in the family responsibilities. Include them in discussions. Be honest with them without telling the nitty-gritty details of why they have only one parent. They need to be able to continue to love their absentee parent.

Children who have been used to two parents will go through natural reactions when one leaves: grief, shock, guilt, rejection, anger, and embarrassment. Some will go through periods of regression to more childish ways. Some will become more silent. Some will blame the parents, and they will transfer their anger to one or both parents.

Negative reactions by the children are to be expected. However, don't overreact, overcompensate, or overprotect them. Be patient. Be a model of understanding. Maintain expectations and disciplines. Have honest discussions, and let time do its healing.

3. *Relationship with friends may change.* Friends of married couples often see their friendship being to the *couple.* They feel threatened when the couple is no longer together. Don't crawl into a hole. Make other friends. Make friends with other families. Don't feel like you are intruding. Give them opportunity to love a single-parent family.

4. *Relationships at work may change.* Both men and women may treat you differently. But don't adopt their stigmatism as yours.

5. *Relationship with family members may change.* It will probably change with the in-laws. But remember they are your children's grandparents, uncles, aunts, etc.

6. *Relationships at church may change.* Some churches still have not accepted divorced people well. We do not often hear prayers asking God to help the single parents or ease their pain. Not many ministers praise from their pulpits the sacrifice that single parents are making. But they ought to. One woman, who was raised from infancy in a small-town church, got her divorce in another community. She thought, "The one place where I can be accepted is back home." But after a year of sitting alone in her hometown church, she moved away.

7. *Household relationships will change.* The traditional male/female responsibilities around the house do not apply to the single person. But don't let new responsibilities change your image of self. See it as expansion, not restriction.

8. *Relations with the neighborhood may change.* Neighbors may relate to you differently. Because of the divorce settlement in regards to the house, or changing jobs (or many other reasons), a divorcee may have to move to a new neighborhood entirely. Make acquaintances in that new neighborhood. Don't see yourself as a *single* person. See yourself as a *person.* Remember everybody is single at one time or another. Be neighborly. Take some goodies to your neighbors. Look after your neighbor's property when they are gone. Don't just expect them to do for you.

The Pain Is Healable

Ask any person who is a single parent and he/she will tell you that the experience is painful. Sometimes the clouds seem so black and the pain so blasting that a person can wonder, "Will I ever be happy again? Will I ever laugh again? Will I ever feel good about myself again?"

Days can pass like years. Every step forward may seem to be followed by ten steps backwards. The emotional anguish can turn into physical sickness. Despair can sometimes be followed by just one thing—more despair.

But God knows what it is like. He went through a divorce himself (Jeremiah 3:8). He has been a single parent since He created man, but He didn't function alone.

He has given us three promises we must never give up believing:

1. "I will *not* leave you orphans. *I* will come to *you.*"

2. "I will be with you *always.*" The "I" is the *personal* God. The "will" is His *persistence.* "Be with" is His *presence.* "You" is the

personableness of His promises. He promises to be with *you*— personally. "Always" is the *perpetuality* of His promise. God doesn't bow out of your life when you are in the pits. In fact, when you feel as if life is caving in, you will find that God is in the cave waiting for you. That's His great promise to you.

3. "God causes *all things* to work together *for good* to those who love God." All things means just that—ALL things.

God opens more doors than He allows to be closed. Keep your eyes open to see what He is opening up for you—new opportunities, new friendships, new tomorrows, a new you, etc.

God doesn't play by the rules we establish. Too often we want to throw in the towel and declare the game over, just because things didn't go the way we had planned. But God declares, "It's not over. Quit blowing the whistle on yourself."

He can always do beyond *all* we ask or think. In fact, He can do *exceeding* abundantly beyond all we can ask or think. He is not limited by our past, and He doesn't want us to be either.

For Consideration or Discussion

Agree or Disagree:
1. "A sign of depression is when we decide unconsciously that it's safer to feel miserable and exhausted than to change." Agree or disagree? Discuss it.
2. Singles are stigmatized in the church. Agree or disagree? Discuss it.
3. Divorced persons tend to move into second marriages too quickly. Agree or disagree? Discuss it.
4. Divorced persons avoid personal relationships because they have lost confidence in their ability to relate. Agree or disagree? Discuss it.
5. Single parents should try to be "a model of understanding" for their children. They will fail to achieve it at times. Agree or disagree? When you fail, what should be your attitude toward the failure? Discuss it.
6. Our church (or group of churches in your area) should have a ministry especially for singles. Agree or disagree? Discuss it.

Grandparenting

10

I saw a plaque at an airport gift shop that read, "Never regret growing old. It's a privilege denied to so many people." People in the western culture, who live past retirement age, are indeed the privileged few compared to others on board the spaceship named "Earth."

Solomon hinted at the privilege of growing older when he wrote, "The honor of old men is their gray hair" (Proverbs 20:29). However not everyone handles the age that comes with graying as a privilege and honor. For many people old age has become something to dread.

Few of us want to become *really* old, even though we *are* getting older every day. Death is the only way to stop it. So why pretend we aren't getting older? Some older people play the "let's pretend" game by acting and dressing like teenagers. Few things are more disgusting than to see grandparents trying to be eighteen-year-olds. Of course, there is nothing wrong with looking the best you can. But some things just can't be painted over or covered up. So live with it, with the attitude that certain identifying marks accompany age. It's not inappropriate to grow older physically.

Getting older is not a license to become cranky. One of the most beautiful sights is a person over sixty with a positive, optimistic, encouraging, open, flexible attitude. Every older person owes the following generation the gift of a good attitude.

Here's a prayer that all of us should try to fulfill.

"Lord, Thou knowest better than I know that I am growing older, and will someday be old. Keep me from getting talkative, and particularly from the fatal habit of thinking I must say something on every subject on every occasion. Release me from the craving to try to straighten out everybody's affairs. Make me thoughtful, but not moody; make me helpful, but not bossy. With my vast store of wisdom, it seems a pity not to use it all, but Thou knowest Lord that I want a few friends at the end of my life. Keep my mind free from recital of endless details. Give me wings to get to the point. Seal my lips on my aches and pains. They are increasing and my love of rehearsing them is becoming sweeter as the years go by. And so I ask for grace, dear Lord. Grace enough to listen to the tales of others' pains and endure them patiently. Teach me the glorious lesson that occasionally it is possible that I may be mistaken. Keep me reasonably sweet. I don't want to be an old saint. Some are so hard to live with but a *sour old person is one of the crowning works of the devil.* Help me to exact all possible fun out of life. There are so many funny things around me, I don't want to miss any of them."

We are doing something in western culture that is detrimental to any culture. Those cultures and subcultures that exist for hundreds and hundreds of years have this philosophy: the older you become the wiser you become, and the more important you are to the rest. But western culture is teaching that the older you get—especially past a certain age—the less important you are, and we really do not need you. A lot of older people have bought that line. Consequently, we are seeing more older people being herded into human junk piles. There they wind away time, as their practicality and wisdom collects rust from nonuse.

Probably the most helpful people we have in our culture are the grandparent kind of people. Someone has observed that becoming a grandparent is God's compensation for growing older. Solomon observed: "Grandchildren are the crown of old men."

Even the church has fallen into this trap. Very seldom do the young and old share in any common church experience. We have split the church into well-defined age groups. If it continues, the young will not glean from the old their valuable heritage, practical experiences, and accumulated wisdom. At the same time, the older do not catch from the younger their creativity, innovations, enthusiasm, and flexibility.

This split-level American society also touches the family. In 1950, fifty percent of American homes had a grandparent living in the same household as grandchildren. But now only two percent of homes have this mix. High mobility has put more and more miles between many grandparents and their grandchildred. Consequently, it takes more consecrated effort to be a functioning grandparent or grandchild today. It is not going to happen just because grandparents and grandchildren live close together, either.

Grandparents have the natural knack of accepting their grandchildren as the most important people in the world, regardless of your batting averages, grades in school, popularity, or always keeping your nose clean. They are not called "grand" parents for no reason.

Age adds to the functionality of grandparents. It doesn't detract from it. To grandparents you can say, and really mean it, "You aren't just getting older; you are getting better."

As I am writing this, my mother is eighty-two-years-old. She is a fantastic functioning grandmother. The 1700 miles that separate us has not discouraged her grandparenting. Last year she came out, by auto, to spend the Christmas holidays with us. And she stayed "on the go" in southern California. She went to Sea World with the grandchildren and loved it. When she went to Knott's Berry Farm, she insisted on riding the parachute jump—twice. She never forgets any of her grandchildren's birthdays or anniversaries. When Valentine's Day rolls around, each of our children gets a little card from my mother. Occasionally, she will stick four sticks of gum in her letters—one stick for each child. But do you know what that says to our kids? It says to them that they are really worth something. They must have value if the lady who is so wise and stable loves them.

There seems to be no generation gap in the appreciations for the input of grandparents. A few years ago, an interesting ad appeared in a classified section of a western newspaper. It included the picture of a darling little girl sitting in a chair with a big smile on her face. Her smile melted your heart. Underneath the picture were these words: "Won't cha be my Grandma or Grandpa?" (Now remember, this is the same section where sofas and cars are advertised for sale.) Then the ad said:

My name is Cherish Dawn. I am 19 months old. I live in Pine Lake. I don't have a Grandma or Grandpa. My Grandfathers had both passed away before I was old enough to say "Grandpa." I don't care if you are bald, fat, skinny, or sick. I can take cookies and share holidays with you. Won't cha be my Grandma or Grandpa? I have a brother 11½, and a sister 10. They are luckier than I. They knew the love and wisdom of a grandparent, but they, too, miss having grandparents."

Love and kisses,
Cherish, Cynthia, and Kevin

Bald, fat, skinny, or sick! Isn't that beautiful?

Later on in the week, the editor of the newspaper had interviewed the mother and wrote an editorial about the ad. After repeating the ad, here's what he wrote:

Elaine Dalmasso believes very firmly that "older people have so much to offer" so that she does not like the idea of her little daughter growing up without having a Grandma and Grandpa. Before her parents passed away several years ago, her other children saw them twice a month, despite the fact that the family home was 800 miles away.

But all that is changed now and the Dalmasso children are not exposed to the input from an older person. So they are looking for a new set of grandparents to fill the void.

The qualifications that Elaine has set are simple: She is looking for a man and a woman over 60 who have no one around them ... It is not necessary that the "grandparents" be married or that they even know each other.

What is important is that they be willing to give the wisdom of their years to three children who will replace it with the joy and happiness of their youth.

"Over 60 who have no one around them." How wonderful! That's the younger generation appreciating the older generation.

A few years ago I was doing a lecture on Staten Island. At the close of the lecture, a man in his fifties came up to me. He had brought his family from the Philippines to this country five years earlier. He was now a successful businessman on Manhattan.

He asked, "Mr. Staton, do you know what I miss most about my homeland?" Big tears welled up in his eyes and started down his cheeks. It had been a long time since I had seen a grown man cry.

I replied, "No, Sir."

He said, "I miss my Grandma. Grandma lived with us, and I grew up sitting on her lap and listening to her advice. The last person I got counsel from before moving my family to this country was Grandma. I miss my Grandmama."

A person doesn't outgrow his respect for grandparents.

A few years ago, while standing in line at a Christian retreat, I began talking to a sweet, dear Christian woman in her eighties. She said to me, "You know, I got a letter from my granddaughter and all it said was, Grandmother, it's so nice to have a friend like you!"

I said, "Isn't that wonderful? How old is your granddaughter?"

"Twenty-five," she said.

"When did she send you that letter?" I asked. I had just assumed it was sent when the granddaughter was a little girl.

"Last week," the grandmother beamed.

From nineteen months to twenty-five-years-old to fifty-years-old, the message is the same: Grandparents are respected. No wonder "Grandchildren are the crown of old men."

However, it isn't enough merely to be a grandparent. It is important to function as one. Here are some functional ideas:

Using the cassette

My grandfathers both died before I was born, but I had wonderful grandmothers. They both died while I was overseas in the service.

Grandparents should get cassette recorders. (If you don't have one, borrow one.) Purchase several cassettes and use them for your grandchildren. Here's a few good uses:

1. *Occasionally send a "cassette letter" to the grandchildren.* Just talk with them on the cassette as you would in a letter. Encourage them to send a "cassette letter" back to you. If they sing or play instruments, ask them to put that on tape.

2. *Share your past with your grandchildren.* Too often we are being cut off from our roots. Many people do not live close to any relatives, so they are not acquainted with their rich heritage. If grandparents feel uncomfortable doing this, because they are not quite sure what to say, then have the children interview them.

Go as far back as your memory can take you. Tell your grand-children about your parents and grandparents, and stories they told you about their past. Talk about life as a little boy or girl. What games did you play? Describe your house, your room, hobbies, etc. Talk about your school. Describe the room and the equipment. How did you get to school? What kind of discipline was used? How was your school heated? Did it have water?

Where did you go courting? How did you get there? What did you do on dates? (Now don't tell everything you did.) Describe the first house you lived in after you got married. Walk through the rooms. Describe the kitchen and appliances. (Our kids need to hear about them. Many believe that God created the automatic washer and dryer on the fifth day.)

Describe the developing days of your grandchildren's parents. As you share your past on tape, also talk about the valleys, the disappointments, the mistakes, etc. Kids need to know that life was not all orchids for you. If they know that you came through questionable days, and how you handled them, that can really be a help.

Also share with them your insights about changing values and morals.

A set of cassette tapes like this would probably be among the most valuable gifts you could leave your grandchildren. The set could be preserved for the generations that follow.

School events

If you live close enough, go to some of the school events of your grandchildren. A couple of years ago I was president of our PTA (which we called community club). We didn't follow traditional PTA meetings. We designated one meeting as Grandparents' Night. We sent special invitations to all grandparents, gave each a certificate of appreciation, had the children sing special songs about grandparents, had a talk about the value of grandparents, etc. From that time on, we had grandparents at every meeting. Grandparents can really be influential with school boards, if they keep up with trends and let their voices be heard. More grandparents need to give their input to board decisions.

Vacation time

Two years ago our family did something we had never done before. We rented a camper and took a vacation. But we also did something else. We invited my in-laws to join us. What a sight— eight of us in a station wagon and eight of us trying to sleep in a pop-up camper. (One of us slept in the wagon each night.)

Taking a vacation with a set of grandparents was about the smartest thing our family has ever done. We had a ball! I will never forget a couple of sights that will always be emotional to me. We were in a mountain cabin for three days. Granddad and Randy went fishing every day. What a sight to see them sitting together in the boat in the middle of a small lake, just taking life easy and enjoying each other. One day as I sat in the living room, I glanced into the kitchen. There was the grandson (inches taller than she) standing next to and talking to his grandmother at the kitchen sink. He had his arm around her. Try a vacation with the grandparents. The grandchildren deserve to taste the multiple, beautiful experiences and the close-up contacts and communications that such an experience offers.

In addition to grandparents taking a vacation with their children and grandchildren, they could invite a grandchild to take a vacation with them. It might be a mini-vacation for just a couple of days. But what a memory that would leave. How about an outing, taking in a ballgame, going to the zoo, amusement park, etc.?

Using the phone

Don't neglect the value of the phone. Even if you live in the same town as your grandchildren, an occasional call can do wonders for tightening up relationships and building self-esteems. A special call for special events such as the first day in kindergarten, commencement, the loss of the first tooth, getting a driver's license, the first week in college, etc., is a great investment.

Using the home

Occasionally invite the grandchildren in for a whole day (or whole week) to live with the grandparents. You might even try a grandchildren's reunion.

A grandchildren's reunion happens when the grandparents invite *all* the grandchildren in at the same time. Don't hesitate to invite a grandchild to join you in a special project, such as baking cookies, going fishing, constructing something, etc.

Following their interests.

If you live in the same town as the grandchildren, try to schedule some time for going to ball games, band concerts, etc. Of course, you can't take them all in! But your presence from time to time can naturally burst the buttons of your grandchildren, and broaden your interests as well.

While many children get the feeling that their parents value their worth by how well they perform, the same children seldom get that feeling from their grandparents. Grandparents have the knack of making the grandchildren feel important regardless of how well or how poorly they perform. At the same time a word of encouragement from grandparents can motivate changed priorities faster than a word from any other person.

Grandparents are the human models of unconditional love. They express love to an imperfect person without that person feeling guilty about receiving the love. "Gray hair" has many advantages. One of them is that the accumulation of years has taught that many things, expectations, accomplishments, performances, etc., are not as important as we thought they were in our younger days.

In his book, *What Wives Wish Their Husbands Knew About Women,* Dr. James Dobson quoted insights about a grandmother from the mind of a nine-year old girl. As you read it, look for a couple of ingredients that are reinforced several times in this writing. That little girl has learned that time is a valuable commodity in the lives of adults. Not many adults have extra time. And when they do, they don't have much time for her. But grandmother has time for her. In fact, just "being there" impresses this little girl. Grandmothers take time in that little girl's world. Here's the article:

> A grandmother is a lady who has no children of her own. She likes other people's little girls and boys. A grandfather is a man grandmother. He goes for walks with the boys, and they talk about fishing and stuff like that. Grandmothers don't have to do anything except to be there. They're old so they shouldn't play hard or run. It is enough if they drive us to the market where the pretend horse is, and have a lot of dimes ready. Or if they take us for walks, they should slow down past things like pretty leaves and caterpillars. They should never say "hurry-up."
>
> Usually grandmotehrs are fat, but not too fat to tie your shoes. They wear glasses and funny underwear. They can take their teeth and gums off.
>
> Grandmothers don't have to be smart, only answer questions like, "Why isn't God married?" and "How come dogs chase cats!"
>
> Grandmothers don't talk baby talk like visitors do, because it is hard to understand. When they read to us, they don't skip or mind if it is the same story over again.

Everybody should try to have a grandmother, especially if you don't have television, because they are the only grown-ups who have time.

Grandparenting is not all one-sided. Grandchildren should take some responsible initiative to maintain relationships. How about writing them letters, calling them, inviting them to *your* home, and remembering their special days? How about taking grandfather fishing for a change?

My mother has one granddaughter who calls her long distance every Saturday. What a beautiful love story that goes on between those two. It's just too easy to let grandparents do all the kind deeds, and then forget about them when they get older and the grandchildren get older. But that's when grandparents need to know that they are loved in special ways. Paul taught that grandchildren should be responsible in providing the material needs of grandparents (1 Timothy 5:4).

Bridging the generation gap with love is a way to erase that gap and to insure the stability of the next generation. The world needs functioning grandparents and grandchildren—and so do you and I.

For Consideration or Discussion

How do you feel about?:
1. How do you feel about growing older?
2. How do you feel about being a grandparent?
3. How do you feel about having/not having living grandparents?
4. How do you feel about the fact that only two percent of American homes have a grandparent living in them as compared to fifty percent in 1950?
5. How do you feel about the way your church ministers to senior citizens?
6. How do you feel about your memories? Share with the group the best experiences you ever had with your grandparents or your most enjoyable memories of them.

Marriage
and Friendships

11

"I've found the person—that one person who can meet all my needs—who can completely fulfill me." Have you ever heard that or thought it? Then forget it. It just isn't true. Each person is so diverse and complex that it takes more than one person to meet *all* the needs of *any* individual. That's why each person needs friends. That's why every marriage needs to allow the married partners to keep friends as well as establish and develop new friends. However, marriages have sometimes done terrible things to friendships in the name of commitment, submission, or love.

When a person will not allow his mate to spend time with friends, the real issue is jealousy not love. Real love is not jealous (1 Corinthians 13:4). Recently I spent a few days in the home of a minister and his wife. The couple had been married for twenty years. I could tell immediately that there was some friction between the two. And there was. The couple openly talked about it with me.

The wife had recently crawled outside the shell of her world which had been very small. Her total interests and activities had centered around the family and her husband. She had begun to make friends and reach out to them. As she did so, her personality blossomed. She had become radiant. She even lost some weight and purchased some new clothes.

Her friends were not manipulative of her time, neither did they demand that she give them priority. But they did begin to confide in her and receive counsel from her. The husband was having trouble handling it. Up to this time he had been her center. And he thought that friends in her life would shut him out. So he was threatened. In fact, he was so threatened that he did not want her to have any friends of the opposite sex. That was one of the first questions they asked me, "Can or should married people be friends with the opposite sex?"

Being committed to one another as husband and wife does not mean we should cut ourselves off from the world. The more we do that, the more we will use and abuse each other. We will restrict the other person from receiving the kind of growth aids that come from many sources.

Instead of relationships which seal us off from others, we need relationships with other people who can be real friends. They will help us be more what we can be. Then we will have more of self to contribute to the mate. The truth is that when you are married you need friends more, not less. A lot of what I receive from my wife—her wholesomeness, her spontaneity, her positive optimism—is in her largely because of her interchange with her friends. In reality, her friends minister to me through my wife; and they do not even know it. You have more to give to one person when you receive more from many.

Love is not like a rifle that can be aimed in only one direction, and fired toward only one target. It is more like a rock that is dropped into a pool of water. Although it hits one spot, the effects spread into every direction simultaneously.

Our super independent society, that worships the "go-aholic" mentality, has de-emphasized friendships to the detriment of us all. We've done it in several ways:

1. *Emphasizing a freedom which weakens commitment.* Friendships demand commitment.

2. *Emphasizing success.* The success syndrome places too many expectations on people. We need to lower our expectations of people. No one is perfect. So don't expect it.

3. *Emphasizing a pleasure.* This has caused us to run away from any experience that hurts, and friends can hurt. But we must be willing to take both the bitterness and benefits that come in the package of friendship. It is costly to have friends, but it is more costly not to.

4. *Emphasizing acceptance.* We stress self-esteem and acceptance so much that people wear eternal masks. We purposely hold ourselves off from making friends, because we do not want them to really get to know us. The only way we can have friends is if we are willing to fail with them, and if we need forgiveness from time to time.

A magazine article of a few years ago described a primitive tribe

104

whose members wore their portraits on their foreheads. They bowed to each other's picture instead of the real person. Don't we tend to do that too much? We've got to take down the portraits we want others to see so they can see us. Then they can be friends to a real person, not a mere image.

What can friendships do for marriage?

1. *Help each individual become more of self.* Friends can draw out of us potentials that have been locked up and just waiting for the key to let them out. When the potentials are drawn out, they can be shared with the mate.

2. *Give stability to the self and to the marriage.* The more friends a person has, the broader is his check and balance against immorality. It is easier to commit immorality with no friends around, for there are fewer people to disappoint.

3. *Allow each mate to see himself through the eyes of others.* Then we see more clearly. The better you see yourself, the better you can see others.

4. *Give each mate more people to open up to and share with.* This alone can help foster better communication at home.

5. *Give each mate needed "shock absorbers" when life at home is bumpy.* Without friends there is no ease from the bumps.

6. *Help develop the personality of the individual.* That developing personality is shared with the mate.

7. *Give the individual an outlet for interests, discussions, etc.* that the mate may not be interested in at this time in his life.

8. *Give the individual outlets for giving himself to the needs of others.* Don't look for only friends that can meet your needs. Look also for those who have needs you can meet.

9. *Help develop the ability to forgive.* A marriage cannot continue without forgiveness. We learn about forgiveness first of all outside the marriage. We need to continue to augment the experiences outside the marriage as well as within it.

With forgiveness, we are liberated to be genuine. Without forgiveness, people can co-exist only if they are cautiously superficial. Too many times we live "surface" lives, so we won't disappoint someone. But disappointments come in interpersonal relationships. Friendships help us to be more realistic about them. Friendships can help us develop forgiveness to others so that we can be more naturally expressive to our mates when they hurt us.

Wrongdoing cannot be avoided, so forgiveness should not. Here are some principles for a forgiving relationship:

1. *Stop blaming the other,* and accept your part in the problem.

2. *See the other's repentance as genuine.*

3. *Let the past be the past.* You can't redo it, so why recycle it through your minds. Be free from it. Then you can be free to relate to people as people of the present.

4. *Be willing to risk being hurt again.* This involves trust. If we live with suspicious fears, we hold the future back and spoil the present. Forgiving is letting what was be gone, and letting what will come come. We do this without our fears that prevent us from entering into the future with caring.

Relationships can be restored only as the wronged person accepts the repentance and the future intentions of the offender as genuine. The forgiving experiences that happen in friendships need to also be poured into marriages.

However, there are some cautions. Do not allow relationships with friends to take priority over the mate. Do not grow so fast in friendships that your mate feels he is left out of your world. Include him. Do not develop the capacity to talk amicably with friends, but not develop amicable talk with your mate. It's interesting how some people can talk hours with friends but not even minutes with their mates. Do not have one tone of voice for friends and another for your mate. Do not allow talk with friends of the oppostie sex to ever include sexual suggestions.

Here are some needs people have in friends. When these are met, they can become more naturally the life-style in a marriage.

1. *An open ear.* An ear that will listen without the other person having to edit what he says.

2. *An accepting spirit.* A person who will continue to accept the friend, even though the friend has really goofed.

3. *An authentic self.* The acceptive spirit frees people to be authentic. Acceptance helps people to be safe while being themselves.

4. *A closed mouth with an open mind.* A person who can listen without feeling he has to preach a sermon or control the other person. The closed mouth also involves a person who will not pass on to anyone else what has been discussed.

5. *A feeling person.* A person who listens with feeling not just with ears. He really cares.

6. *A sacrificial person.* A person who will go out of the way to help a friend.

7. *A receiving person.* A person who receives help, gifts, etc., not somebody who is always giving. To always insist on giving, puts

the other person into an inferior position that is very uncomfortable.

8. *A forgiving person.* A person who will not keep score on hurts.

9. *A truthful person.* A person who can shoot from the shoulder as well as from the heart. Phonies do not help us grow.

10. *A kind person.* Someone who is considerate, not competitive. Truthfulness does not give us a license to purposely hurt people with our tongues.

There is too much tongue damage done in a marriage. Perhaps real close friendships developed outside the marriage would help tame the tongue inside it. Too often we cut down in an effort to get self-acceptance. But the experiences of friendships reduce the need for self-acceptance at the expense of others.

Friends who meet the above needs do immeasurable value to any marriage.

Marriage partners who will not permit their mates to develop friendships are hurting their mates, themselves, their children—and the community at large. More friends need to live in a community.

Making and keeping friends requires some active doing on our part. It requires the following:

1. *Invest time.* Friends take time.
2. *Give energy.* Friends can drain energy, but they are worth it.
3. *Set a priority.* We can't put this way down the line.
4. *Take risks.* Be willing to do that.
5. *Forgive.*
6. *Don't be surprised* when friends disappoint you.
7. *Think the best* about them, but be realistic.
8. *Understand them.* We love each other better when we understand.
9. *Talk openly,* not just about things and people, but also ideas and feelings.
10. *Be willing* to drop-in and be dropped-in on without announcement. Spontaneity is crucial to friendships.
11. *Eat with them.*
12. *Be interruptible.*
13. *Go out of your way to care.*
14. *Share good reading,* and other good experiences with them.
15. *Be transparent,* but do not share negative thoughts about people. Don't poison the minds of your friends against other people.
16. *Allow them room to have other friends.* Don't dominate

their time and affection so much that you keep them squeezed in to just you.

17. Don't be a pest.
18. *Don't keep score* on what you've done for them.
19. *Don't pass on tidbits* about your friends.
20. *Protect your friend's psychological,* spiritual, intellectual, and social needs.
21. *Be patient.*
22. *Don't insist on your own way* all the time.
23. *Don't think you are superior* or inferior to them.
24. *Hang in there,* even when they are not friendly.
25. *Be available.*

One of the needs of the church is for members to become better friends with each other. But that will never happen if Christian marriages veto friendships outside the marriage. Christian families need to help the church become God's family of friends.

For Consideration or Discussion

Friendship quotient:
1. I have many good friends. Yes_____ No_____
2. I have a few very close friends. Yes_____ No_____
3. When I meet with my friends, they do most of the talking. Yes_____ No_____
4. When a friend confides in me, I keep it to myself. Yes_____ No_____
5. I frequently take the initiative in arranging social occasions with friends. Yes_____ No_____
6. I give special attention to my friends when they are in difficulty. Yes_____ No_____
7. When new people attend church, I take the initiative in greeting them and getting to know them. Yes_____ No_____
8. I congratulate my friends on happy occasions, and I comfort them at times of sadness. Yes_____ No_____
9. I try to have some friends whose values and life-styles are different from mine. Yes_____ No_____
10. When a friend disappoints me, I remain a friend. Yes_____ No_____

Each statement is worth 10 points for each "yes" answer. One should score at least 70 for an "average" friendship quotient.

Sex and Spirituality

12

Can you be interested in sex and spirituality at exactly the same time in your bedroom? An odd question? Aren't sex and spirituality two opposites? Isn't it a bit embarrassing to have them connected?

Not at all. One of the spiritual ministries married partners can share with each other is sexual intimacy. How can something so physical have spiritual significance to it? Easy! Spiritual ministries normally come through some kind of physical activity. The Lord's Supper is quite physical—physical drink, bread, plates, and cups. But it has significant spiritual dimensions. Baptism is very physical, but with spiritual ministry. From our dimension, fellowshipping together is physical but it carries grand benefits in Christianity.

So it is with sexual intimacy between a husband and wife. It is physical, but with significant spiritual services. However, before further development, I need to ask you a couple questions. (1) Who designed this whole idea of sex? God did! (2) Who has the cleanest/purist mind that has ever existed? God.

Consequently, out of the cleanest mind that has ever or will ever exist came the whole idea of sexual intimacy. If we automatically conclude that sex is dirty, we are doing something very unkind to God's creative design of our bodies and emotions.

We are "God-*ufactured*" people. God designed sex with His "God-*ufactured*" designs of us in mind. Sex has been given to us for our good, because He loves us.

The Corinthians had a tough time understanding that, and so do some of us. Corinth was a pagan city, and sexual perversions were done as part of the worship of pagan deities. One such "deity" was Aphrodite, the goddess of love. The religion expressed honor to Aphrodite by having males and females on duty in the temple area for intercourse with worshipers.

People who grew up in that kind of religion and became Christians, began to have a hard time separating *any* sexual activity from perverted paganism. Consequently, they began to think that Christians should not share sexual intimacies with their mates. It was just too "dirty" for Christians.

Don't think that's farfetched. Today we live in a very sexually perverted society. Many people hear the word "sex" only with an "X-rated" mentality. Because of this, many Christians come to marriage very reluctant about the beauty of sexual intimacy. Few see it as a spiritual ministry.

Although the Corinthian Christians thought they should abstain from sexual intimacy with their mates, their bodies were having a tough time agreeing with their minds. So they wrote to Paul for advice.

Their position was that it was good for a husband not to touch a wife (1 Corinthians 7:1). Paul did not agree. In fact He said the opposite, "Let each man have his own wife, and let each woman have her own husband" (1 Corinthians 7:2). The word "have" was one of the words for sexual intimacy in that day. Paul heightened his advice by saying, "Let the husband fulfill his duty to his wife, and likewise also the wife to her husband" (1 Corinthians 7:3). "Duty" is an unfortunate translation of the Greek. The Greek word means to owe someone something. Sexual intimacy is a debt husbands and wives owe to each other.

I don't know about you, but I'm in debt.

But there's one debt I do not mind paying. It's the debt of 1 Corinthians 7:3. I hope my wife doesn't get a stamp made and someday stamp the back of my hand "Paid in Full."

Sexual intimacy is a debt because:
1. It helps complete God's creative design of our mates.
2. It helps protect from Satan.
3. It helps relieve tension.
4. It communicates.
5. It unites.
6. It produces offspring made in the image of God.
7. It gives pleasure.
8. It provides the natural environment for expressing verbal, mutual admiration.

It helps complete God's creative design of our mates. (1 Corinthians 7:4).

When Paul said, "The wife does not have authority over her own

110

body," he was saying that she doesn't have the power to be satisfied in the sexual area by herself. However, "the husband does." He has the power to satisfy her sexually. Likewise, the husband doesn't have the power by himself to be satisfied sexually, but the wife does.

This verse is one of the finest commentaries on Genesis 2:18. There the Lord God said, "It is not good for the man to be alone; I will make him a helper suitable for him." The words "suitable for" come from a Hebrew word which means "corresponds with what is the front of" him. God knew what he placed "in front of" the male, and He created a woman that could physically correspond to that. It is a spiritual ministry to help complete or fulfill God's creative design of our mates. This verse says something important against homosexuality. God created Adam and Eve, not Adam and Steve.

It helps protect from Satan (1 Corinthians 7:5).

"Stop depriving one another, except by agreement," is a command that is just as sacred as Acts 2:38. The word "agreement" comes from the same Greek word for *symphony*. A symphony is an orchestra in which the players play in concord. The instruments harmonize in "agreement." They blend together well.

The word means *mutual* agreement. One partner doesn't have the Biblical right to say night after night, "I'm just too tired," "Good-night," or "I've got a headache."

"Stop depriving one another, except by *(mutual)* agreement for a time that you may devote yourselves to prayer, (Who holds off for *that* reason?) and come together again lest Satan tempt you because of your lack of self-control."

The devil knows how we are made, and he'll take advantage of every opportunity he can. Also, he has a lot of lonely people to use.

To deprive our mate does not mean we will yield to Satan's temptation, but we surely put our mate (and ourselves) into a very vulnerable situation. To share sexual intimacy is one way to help protect our mate and ourselves from the onslaught of the devil. And *that* is a spiritual ministry.

It helps to relieve tension.

All of us are like human teakettles or pressure cookers. Pressure builds in our lives. What happens when a teakettle or pressure cooker is on the burner, and there is no outlet for the buildup to escape. It may eventually blow.

People are like that. We are usually on a burner. Sometimes it may be turned up too high, and sometimes it may be turned too low. Either way, pressure builds in our lives.

God has given us many "God-*ufactured*" outlets such as work, exercise, conversation, worship, etc. One of His designed outlets for us is sexual expression between husband and wife. Outside of marriage, sexual intercourse builds pressure and tension. But within marriage it should help relieve pressures.

The next time your husband comes home from work, and you can tell things haven't gone very well for him, that's the time to put on that special negligee. The next time you men come home, and you notice things haven't gone very well for the wives, that's the time to give her special attention. There is no greater muscle relaxing, and mind settling activity, than to share intimacies.

It communicates.

"Now the man had relations with his wife Eve, and she conceived and gave birth to Cain" (Genesis 4:1). The words "had relations" come from a Hebrew word that literally means "know," which describes what goes on in the intimate love act. It is indeed a way to "know." It is communication and interpersonal reaction that seeks to know and be known beyond surface levels. It is communication shared, not just spoken. The love act is a "talk" that cannot be duplicated in any other way.

It unites.

"For this cause a man shall leave his father and his mother, and shall cleave to his wife; and they shall become one flesh." One of the meanings of "one flesh" is the unity of intercourse between a husband and wife. In intercourse two become united emotionally, mentally, and physically—or should.

Sexual intimacy is not to be an added tack-on. It is a crowning moment that captures the love, appreciation, and mutuality of all the other moments of the day. Sexual intimacy is far more than just the physical act of intercourse. Thus, a meaningful sex life between a husband and wife does not depend only upon how they get into bed at night (or whenever). It depends on how they get out of bed in the morning (or whenever), and their interpersonal relationships with each other all day. It is difficult for one mate (especially the wife) to be ignored or mistreated outside the bedroom and then feel that he/she is not being "used" in the love act.

Give your mate special attention all day, and it's much easier to get attention at night. Your mate has far more to be noticed, massaged, and loved than the body.

112

It produces offspring made in the image of God.

"And God blessed them; and God said to them, 'Be fruitful and multiply, and fill the earth' " (Genesis 1:28).

What a spiritual ministry to humanity—multiplying the image of God. What a ministry to each other—providing another person to love and care for. This has the potentiality of taking our eyes off of self. We become more selfish and mature as we pour ourselves into another developing life.

While producing offspring is *one* reason for sexual intimacy, it is not the *only* reason. If it were, God would probably not have designed woman in such a way that she could conceive only three days a month. He would not have said, "Stop depriving one another."

A woman who cannot conceive a child, or a man who cannot beget one, has no Biblical grounds for thinking he/she is an incomplete person. Being able to conceive or beget has nothing to do with completeness. A few years ago a girl in Indianapolis gave birth to a set of twins that was conceived when she was nine-years-old. Giving birth hardly verifies her completeness as a woman.

More important than whether or not one can conceive or beget is whether or not one is willing to "mother" or "father" a new life.

It gives pleasure.

If most couples were asked, "Is sex a duty, a dread, or a delight?" I wonder how they would respond—particularly the wife. I'm afraid many would say, "It's a dread. You know 'for better or for worse,' and this is one of those worse." Certainly many wives would think this way if they believe the only reason for the sex act is to have children.

But it doesn't have to be a dread. God wants it to be a delight. He created sex partly for pleasure, but not selfish pleasure—for mutual recreation, not just for procreation. We see this dimension being expressed by Sarah. When Sarah was eighty-nine-years old, she received the news that she was going to have a baby—her *first*.

She "laughed to herself" (Genesis 18:12). Laughed? That's right! Why? Because she was old? That's hardly the reason to laugh. There's more to it. "After I have become old, shall I have pleasure, my lord being old also?" The word "pleasure" is one of the Hebrew descriptions for the sex act between a husband and wife Sarah's laugh must have been a delightful anticipation of the love-sharing act with her husband. She saw that as pleasure. What

113

a fantastic response! She could never have responded with *that* word had she and her husband not allowed that dimension of their life together to be pleasurable. It calls for mutual caring and sharing in meeting the other person's needs—*agape* love.

It provides the natural environment for expressing verbal mutual admiration.

Nonverbal ways of saying "I love you" need to be backed up with verbal expressions of love. The bedroom intimacies between a husband and wife provide the natural environment for the verbal expressions of appreciation.

Nowhere do we see this better than in the *Song of Solomon*. The entire Bible book records the admiration that a husband and wife have for each other. Every married person ought to read it with the question, "How long has it been since I've talked with my mate like that?" Here are just a few of the gems from that book:

Wife: "May he kiss me with the kisses of his mouth! For your love is better than wine (1:2)." That's like saying today, "Your love (bedroom manners) is more refreshing than cool drink."

Wife: "Your oils have a pleasing fragrance" (1:3). She won't say that to us if we don't shower, use deodorant, and after-shave lotion.

Husband: "To me, my darling, you are like my mare among the chariots of Pharoah" (1:9). We need to make some changes due to different cultures. I wouldn't dare say to my wife, "Darling, you remind me of an old horse." While animals were precious then, today it may be cars. Do our wives see us appreciating them more than the Pintos, Colts, Mustangs, Jaguars, etc.?

Husband: "How handsome you are, my beloved, and so pleasant! Indeed, our couch is luxuriant!" (1:16). Isn't their mutual admiration beautiful to read about?

Wife: "Like an apple tree among the trees of the forest, so is my beloved among the young men. In his shade I took great delight and sat down, and his fruit was sweet to my taste" (2:3). Here's a wife totally satisfied with her husband. She compares the bedroom to a banquet hall. It's enjoyable. "He has brought me to his banquet hall, and his banner over me is love" (2:4).

Husband: "Your hair is like a flock of goats that have descended from Mount Gilead" (4:1). We'd better change something here. I wouldn't dare say, "Darling, your hair looks like a bunch of goats." Perhaps, "Your hair is like mink and silk merged together." For several verses the husband praises his wife's body. Do we?

Husband: "You have made my heart beat faster, my sister, my bride; you have made my heart beat faster with a single glance of your eyes, with a single strand of your necklace" (4:9). Here's a guy about to have a cardiac arrest over his own wife. Fantastic!

Wife: "I am my beloved's, and his desire is for me" (7:10).

All of the *Song of Solomon* reads like this. But why is it in the Holy Bible? Because it's the kind of model relationship God would like to see happen between every husband and wife.

Neither mate should ever use sex as a means to get his way. Their bodies belong to each other. If one keeps it from the other, that one is stealing from the other. If a woman uses sex to induce her mate to buy her a new coat, or make a decision in her favor, she is functioning with a prostitute mentality. Sex is lowered to the *eros* (selfish) level, rather than the *agape* (self-giving) level. All sexual expressions should be filled with agape love, each person meeting the needs of the other. This calls for understanding what excites and pleases the other. It calls for patience and care. It calls for not insisting on your own way (1 Corinthians 13:4-7).

Although sexual expression as an expression of love is normal and right within marriage, some guidelines are necessary. This is mentioned because of some false teaching concerning the application of Hebrews 13:4, which reads: "Let marriage be held in honor among all, and let the marriage bed be undefiled; for fornicators and adulterers God will judge." This verse teaches that neither marriage nor the marriage bed is to be downgraded. Before the first century ended, some leaders were teaching that Christians should neither marry (1 Timothy 4:3) nor have intimacy if they were married. The writer of Hebrews denies both positions.

The misapplication of Hebrews 13:4 stems from the problem of the text itself. The words "let" and "be held" are not in the original manuscript. This makes for two possible readings, the one quoted above and this one: "Marriage is honorable in everything." Those who support this reading apply the words "in everything" to all varieties of sexual expression between husband and wife. They say that no matter what happens between the husband and wife in the

115

bed, the bed is undefiled. This is basically true; however, some use this interpretation to force their mates into all kinds of unpleasantries without mutual consent or mutual fulfillment. Some psychologists use this text to advocate sexual perversions to which the wife especially must submit.

The immediate context, "Let marriage be held in honor and let the marriage be undefiled" makes better reading, because of the word "for" that follows. For God will condemn the immoral and adulterous. The marriage bed certainly is not undefiled in everything, because immorality and adultery are immediately excluded.

The word for "marriage bed" is *koite,* from which our English word "coitus" comes. Coitus refers to the natural conveying of semen to the female reproductive tract. (See Leviticus 15:16ff.) Hebrews 13:4 is saying, "Let natural sexual expression, which is intercourse, be undefiled." When would it be defiled? By adultery or sexual perversion.

When would there be sexual perversion between the husband and wife? Rather than list any specific acts, I would suggest that perversion is any act that degrades the beauty, the unity, and the love of the intimacy. I suggest the following criteria to determine when this happens: (1) When the act of sex is for selfish gratification only, without concern for the other's need; (2) when it is not an act of unity; that is, when both do not voluntarily give themselves to each other; (3) when one mate exploits the other. Between married partners, attitudes defile more than acts.

No mate has the right to force the other. We are to love persons, not practices. We must control the passions, not let passions control us! Sexual intimacies between husband and wife need not be restricted to just one kind (intercourse), but both mates should mutually share in the expressions of any itimacy in *agape*-love. There are three possible levels of sexual expression within marriage: the instinct level (selfish pleasure), the duty level, and the agape level (seeing a need and moving to meet it).

On the agape level, each mate learns how the other is fulfilled and has the patience needed to fulfill those needs. Husbands and wives must discuss openly how each is stimulated in sexual intimacy. Real lovemaking is giving, not just receiving.

I am convinced that few *sex problems* exist between husbands and wives, but there are many *self problems.* Compatibility and fidelity in sex begin with the Holy Spirit who frees people to live for others.

Some Practical Suggestions

1. Every married couple should read some good books dealing with sexuality in a marriage. Here is a partial list:

John E. Eichenlaub, M.D., *The Marriage Art*

John E. Eichenlaub, M.D., *New Approaches to Sex in Marriage*

Tim and Beverly LaHaye, *The Act of Marriage*

Herbert J. Miles, M.D., *Sexual Happiness in Marriage*

Charlie and Martha Shedd, *Celebration*

Ed Wheat, M.D., and Gaye Wheat, *Intended for Pleasure*

2. Don't just read; discuss and experiment.

3. Openly discuss with each other likes and dislikes about sexual intimacy.

4. Ask your husband for enough money to buy seven different negligees. If you can't get that much, then get enough money for one. Buy the most exciting one you can find. Don't just buy it—wear it.

5. Get away from the house, kids, and responsibilities for a weekend affair with your mate.

6. Plan to go to bed at nine o'clock, but agree together that you do not intend to go to sleep until 11.

7. Now check your watch. How much time is left until nine? Start planning!

For Consideration or Discussion

True or False:

1. The Bible says masturbation is a sin.   T   F
2. The Bible says oral sex is a sin.   T   F
3. The Bible says sexual desire is a sin.   T   F
4. Men are more interested in sex than women.   T   F
5. The Bible says unmarried couples may have sexual intercourse if they love each other.   T   F
6. In a healthy marriage, couples will engage in sexual intercourse at least once a week.   T   F
7. The Bible forbids the use of contraceptive devices.   T   F
8. The Bible teaches that the purpose of sexual intercourse is primarily to have children, and only secondarily for pleasure.   T   F
9. The Bible teaches that adultery is the unpardonable sin.   T   F

10. The Bible teaches that one should divorce a spouse who has committed adultery.   T   F
11. The Bible teaches that petting between two married persons is a sin.   T   F
12. Men experience sexual pleasure and fulfillment in marital sexual intercourse much easier than do women.   T   F
13. Men should usually take the initiative in marital sexual intercourse.   T   F
14. Single and celibate persons can be more spiritual than married persons.   T   F
15. Everyone who is married or plans to be married should read one of the recommended books on sexuality listed in this chapter.   T   F

Answers are printed upside down below.

1. False.   The Bible does not discuss masturbation.
2. False.   The Bible does not discuss oral sex.
3. False.   The Bible says "lust" is a sin. Lust is difficult to define. It is here defined as sexual arousal toward a person not one's spouse, with intent to act out that arousal if possible. Sexual desire is a function of our created human nature and it is described as "good" in the book of Genesis.
4. False.   No studies support generalization.
5. False.   See Hebrews 13:4 and 1 Corinthians 6:9-11.
6. False.   Studies show that frequency of intercourse may vary widely.
7. False.   The Bible does not discuss it.
8. False.   The Bible indicates that sexual intercourse is an expression of the relationship of the couple.
9. False.
10. False.   The Bible teaches that one may divorce an adulterous spouse, but that they also may forgive that spouse.
11. False.   The Bible does not discuss it.
12. False.   Although men are usually more easily aroused sexually, and more quickly satisfied sexually, once a woman is aroused her sexual experience may be more intense and prolonged than is a man's.
13. False.   If you said "true," you are expressing a cultural sterotype about gender roles.
14. False.   See 1 Timothy 4:1-5.
15. True.

118

Parents' Greatest Investment —Time

13

It is not easy being a parent in today's society. Neither the mother nor the father has a corner on easiness. Many women are functioning as both mother and father in the home. It is super tough being a wife and mother today. Outside sources are programming frustration into women by telling them that it restricts their potentiality to be "domestic engineers." It is really boring, frustrating, dumb, and noncreative to be a housewife and mother?

My wife is one sharp cookie. She says that being a housewife and mother is the most unrestrictive and creative way she can reach toward her potentialities. As a housewife and mother, she can move into and out of many different kinds of activities. She can be an MD and an RN. She can teach kindergarten, junior high, and high school without anyone checking up on her credentials. She can be an interior decorator, she can be a fashion consultant. (I never go out in public without my wife putting my clothes together.)

Julia can be an editor. I never send anything off for publishing (and this is our twenty-third book) without her editing it. She can be a counselor, Little League behind-the-scenes worker, a taxicab driver, and a music critic. She can also be a defense attorney, prosecuting attorney, judge, jury, and executor—all within three minutes.

However, it isn't all creativity and variety. There are the daily humdrum chores—meals, cleaning, and laundry—more laundry—and still more laundry. (How did our mothers and grandmothers make it by washing just once a week. I know we didn't change clothes as often, but I can't figure out how we stood the smell.) There are many days when the wife does not look into the mirror and say, "Ah—the total woman." Instead she looks and says, "Oh, no! The *totaled* woman."

A wife who is at home needs some relief. Recent studies have revealed that gorilla mothers in capitivity have a habit of eventually abusing and rejecting their babies, but gorilla mothers in their natural habitat never do. What's the difference? The difference is that out in the wilds the other family members—father, grandparents, aunts, uncles, etc. sense when the mother has "had it" with her children and they relieve her.

Have you ever "had it" with your children at home? Did you ever want to scream or throw the kids out the window—or jump out of it yourself? That's the time for relief. But in our society of high mobility, we are often miles away from support family members. That's one reason establishing friendships are more important in a mobile society. Sunday-school classes ought to be sensitive to the parenting pressures of young couples. Sunday-school classes of older members could offer young parents a night of free child care a month. Why not volunteer to stay all night with the children and let that couple get away alone? If they can't afford a motel, let them stay at your house for the night. We all need an oasis.

That oasis should also come from the father who comes home at night. He does not come home just to be served as the king of his castle, but to give some relief to the queen. She has been with children all day. Now she needs an adult in her world to communicate with and to do some things with. She also needs time by herself. She may need to go shopping, spend some time with girl friends, etc. The father needs to spend time with the children. If he doesn't, the home has a man in it but not a father.

It is important for the husband to allow his wife to develop relationships with friends. In our society there seems to be a trend away from close friendships. Areas of the country that say "hi there" to strangers are sometimes the most difficult areas in which to develop close friends. A newcomer is still seen as an "outsider" twenty years later and the friendship is still at the level of "hi there." We often run away from what we most need—close friends. A real friend is someone who knows all about you, accepts you not only for your strengths, but is also willing to embrace your weaknesses. Deep, meaningful relationships help the most difficult days pass with lessened strain. Telling a friend about your mistakes helps to dispel guilt, inadequacy, and shame. It adds to a person's health. That's why God taught us to confess to one another. Sharing the joys of life helps make those moments all the more precious. Many couples need to work hard to establish friendships outside their marriage.

120

It is also important for the husband to give the wife money to buy new clothes (as the budget permits), or money to eat out occasionally with a girl friend (as the budget permits) without being threatened or jealous. This does not give the wife the right to become arrogantly independent. It is to recognize that she is made in the image of God, with her own uniqueness and personality that needs to be expressed and developed beyond only her identity with her husband and children. The wife is a helper fit for her husband. The husband who will not allow his wife's God-given potentialities to emerge is restricting the kind of help that is fit for him. We must never equate a submissive wife with a suppressed wife. Legalism will do that, but love will not. The husband is given the mandate to love his wife as Christ loved the church. Loving the church, Christ frees her to become what she can become.

So it is to be in a marriage. The husband should encourage his wife to develop and express her potentialities as a person, and to see this development as a complement to him rather than as competition to him. Our society is worsened when a woman's individuality is suppressed in her submission. We can only guess how much better our world could be if women's creativity were shared in many areas of life.

However, parents can be so busy providing outlets to each other in developing self-potentiality and self-esteem that the children get left out. The older I get, the more I am convinced that it is not the amount of money we invest in our children that impresses them, but the amount of time we invest in their lives. I used to say, "It's quality time, not quantity time that counts." But that is just a psychological rationalization for putting the kids on the back burner. We don't say that about other areas of our life. Try saying that about the farm or garden and see what happens. Try taking care of the house or cooking with that philosophy. Try showing up for work with that idea.

Ken Chafin tells about the time he came home for dinner and his little daughter exictedly asked, "Daddy, are you going to be able to stay home tonight?" He had to say, "No, Honey, tonight I have to go talk to some men about how to be a good daddy." Tears started to come to the little girl's eyes. Dr. Chafin then said, "Honey, while we are eating dinner tonight, would you tell me what a good daddy is? And I'll tell those men what you say."

Several times during dinner she would get up out of her chair, walk over to her dad, and whisper something into his ear. Each time she did, Chafin wrote something down on a piece of paper. Later on that evening as he got up to speak, he pulled a little piece of paper out of his pocket. On it was written, "How to be a good Daddy:

1. Watch a fish.
2. Build a fire.
3. Fly a kite.
4. Catch a butterfly.
5. Plant a flower.
6. Get a kitty cat out of the mud."

As far as that little girl was concerned, that was it. But do you see what she was saying? Being a good daddy doesn't require all the big dreams and projects we may think about. It's the little things that make the difference.

I don't remember much about growing up before I was five-years-old, but I remember one incident as if it had happened yesterday. One Saturday morning my dad took me to a cattle auction in Danville, Illinois. I don't remember a thing about the cattle auction, but here's what I do remember. There was a restaurant filled with important men. For a little four-year-old boy, every grown man is important. But my dad and I were together, sitting on stools drinking root beer. I'll never forget it. In the midst of busy, important men, my dad had time for a little kid like me. It is the little things we do, not just the big things we do, that make an impression on our children's lives. If you look back upon your life as a little boy or little girl growing up, it is the little things that you remember that mean so much to you now.

A man out in Oregon came up to me some time ago and said, "Let me tell you what I remember about growing up. I lived on a farm. Often my dad would come home, take his coat off, put it at the door, kick off his boots, and sit down at the kitchen table. Sometimes he'd slap his knee and say, 'Come here, Son.' And I'd sit on his lap. He would put his arms around me, and we'd just talk for a few moments." He said, "That's what I remember about a boy growing up."

I'll never forget something that happened several years ago when Randy was about five years of age. He was helping me work in the morning. We were washing the car together, and we knocked off about noon. I took a shower and went down to the study to work on an assignment for a convention. Randy came in. He said, "Dad, could you and I do something together?" And I said, "Son, we

122

spent all morning doing something together." Then Randy answered me with something that you will not find in a psychology book, but he was absolutely on target. He said, "But, Daddy, this morning I was doing something with you, and now I'd like for you to do something with me." Do you see what he thought? While I thought I was doing things with him, he visualized being up in a man's world. Now he wanted me to do something with him down in his world.

It's the little things that we can do with our kids that count. In one city where I was speaking, a teacher came up to me and said, "Let me tell you what happened in our school. A teenage boy had gotten into trouble. It was about the second or third time, so we called his dad in. I, the principal, and the dad and the boy met together. The father and the son were not belligerent with each other, but the father said, 'I can't understand why my boy keeps getting into trouble. I give him everything.' Then the son turned to the dad and said, 'No, Dad, you really don't.' And the father said, 'What do you mean, Son?' The son said, 'Do you remember how you used to tell me about Grandpa helping you build a sled? Dad, you have never helped me build a sled, or done anything with me. You've always given it to me.' " From that day on, the relationship between that boy and his dad became different the teacher said.

Another time a man came up to me and said, "Let me tell you something that happened in our family. My dad was a politician, and he had just made the announcement he was going to run for reelection. That was big news. TV cameras came into the house and the crew set up. They were going to do a news special on my dad running for reelection. While the TV cameras were getting set up, the director of the crew came over to me and said, 'We'd like to do a shot of you and your dad doing something together. What do you and your dad do together?' I said, 'Well, my dad and I never do anything together.' And he said, 'Oh!' So they made up something and did the shot of it." When the TV crew tore down and left, the father came up to that little boy, who was about ten-years-old, and said, "Son, I heard what you said to the TV man, and I've been thinking about that ever since. You're right! We haven't done anything together. I'm going to back out of this election, and I'm going to get involved in something else so that you and I can do some things together." And he did. (That thirty-year-old son was in church that night, and I really believe that was his sitting-on-the-stool, drinking-a-nickel-root-beer-experience.)

As a busy man, I don't have time to direct the carnival for the PTA, but as a father I take the time. As a busy man, I really don't have time to go to Cub Scout meetings. When our son was in Cub Scouts, and I went to a meeting, I thought I'd just invaded the county women's sewing club! I was the only man there. And as a busy man, I don't have time to be going to Peewee League ball games, or Little League ball games, or girls' softball games. As a father, I take the time.

I'll never forget when Randy got into Peewee League. I didn't play ball when I was growing up. We were very poor, so I started to work when I was in the sixth grade, and I worked till midnight every night. Randy tried out for Peewee League when he was six years of age, and he got to be catcher. I went out immediately and bought two ball gloves—one for him and one for me. I didn't know till the next week that a catcher has a special mitt. So I bought three ball gloves that summer.

I have missed very few ball games. It's a family affair as a matter of fact. We take the whole family. Once when our kids had chicken pox we went! The girls sat all the way on the other side of the field in front of the car.

I discovered at those games that I was about the only man around, so I decided to try and out yell every woman. You folks know how loud mothers can yell at ball games? When those kids had chicken pox, and Julia was on the other side of the field, as we got in the car after that game she said, "Buddy, do you know how loud you yell?" I said, "No." She said, "You're the only person we could hear. You're obnoxious!" (I tried to tone it down just a little bit after that.)

But, men, you've got to program priority time with the kids, or it just will not get done. You can use dead time. By that I mean time that isn't really planned for anything else—like going to town or going to the store. I say, "Kids, do you want to go with me?" You can talk a lot to the kids when they're just riding with you in the car.

I was scheduled to speak up in Canada a couple of years ago. I looked at my schedule and realized that I could drive up there, although I don't *like* to drive that kind of distance. I thought, "I think I'll drive and take the kids." What a delightful time! We put sleeping bags and bicycles in the back of the station wagon. We got up early in the morning so we could knock off about two-thirty in the afternoon and go swimming. What a precious way to spend time with the kids.

124

Some things I read a few years ago caused me to change some of my priorities. I had to work hard at doing it. Let me share with you what some of those things were. One was a poem entitled, "Tomorrow, I'll Be Big." On it was a picture of a boy on a tricycle out in a field. I've put my son's name in it. It says:

If only he'd just said once,
   "Okay, Randy, let's do it together today."
But it's always tomorrow:
   "Tomorrow, son, hey, let's do it tomorrow.
   I'm busy today."
But tomorrow I'll be big, Daddy.
I'm only little now. Now is when I need you.
I wonder if I could try another approach?
I've got it. I'll go away and become a stranger
   because my dad always has time for strangers.
No, no, that'll take too much time.
I'll make an appointment, 'cause my dad will
   always keep appointments.
Aw, shucks, why go to all of that bother?
I think I'll try the other approach one more time.
"Daddy, could you and I do something together today?
Tomorrow I'll be big, and Daddy,
   I need you and I love you."

About that time my wife cut out a cartoon from a Sunday paper and gave it to me. Frame number one: Ditto said, "Dad, could you and I shoot the BB gun together?" And the father said, "No, Son, not today because I've got to get this report done." Ditto said, as boys will often do, "Well, Dad, when you and Mom get home from shopping, could you and I just do something together?" He said, "Not today, Son, I've got to mow the yard." In the next to the last frame, little Ditto was walking down the hall to his room. He had his hands in his pockets and his head down. He was saying, "Gee, I wish Daddy could learn there's more to being a daddy than making excuses."

A few years ago *Reader's Digest* condensed a book by John Dreschner entitled, *If I Were Starting My Family Again.* Here are some things he said he would do differently.

   1. *I would love my wife more.* It's just too easy to take

family members for granted. Dreschner said that he would be freer in letting his children see him love their mother. He would show more little kindnesses, such as place her chair at the table, give her gifts, write her letters, etc.

2. *I would develop feelings of belonging.* If a child does not feel that he belongs to the family, he will soon find his primary group elsewhere. It is possible that people who live in the same house are really existing worlds apart. We need to use mealtimes more for sharing. We need to play games more. When a child feels he belongs to the family, he has a stability that can more easily stand the taunts of the gang and the temptations of the world.

3. *I would laugh more with my children.* Dreschner said, "I see now that I was, many times, too serious. While my children loved to laugh, I, too often must have conveyed the idea that being a parent was a perennial problem."

4. *I would be a better listener.* "To most of us, a child's talk seems like unimportant chatter. Yet, I now believe, there is a vital link between listening to the child's concerns when he is young and the extent to which he will share his concerns with his parents when he is in his teens.

   "If my children were small again, I'd be less impatient if they interrupted my newspaper reading. There's a story about a small boy who tried repeatedly to show his father a scratch on his finger. Finally his father stopped reading and impatiently said, "Well, I can't do anything about it, can I?" "Yes, Daddy," the boy said. "You could have said, 'Oh.' "

5. *I would do more encouraging.* Encouragement helps children more than faultfinding and criticism. Each of us craves to be appreciated. We will live up to or down to how we think others see us and believe in us. Dreschner said. "So, if I were starting my family again, I would persist in daily praise, seeing not only what the child is now, but what he can be."

6. *I would seek to share God more intimately.* There is a story that tells about a little boy who awoke in the

middle of the night afraid of the lightning he saw and the thunder he heard. "Daddy, come, I'm scared." "Son," the father said, "God loves you and He'll take care of you." "I know God loves me," the boy replied, "but right now I want somebody who has skin on."

Many people who read this cannot restart their families. And many may say, "I have really goofed it." But God's grace can overcome any goof we have made. This is not the time to drown ourselves in guilt. It is the time to give ourselves and our families to the grace of God.

Others reading this still have children at home. They do not need to say, "If I were starting my family again." Instead they can say, "I can start doing differently—and I'm going to."

For Consideration or Discussion

1. Take each one of your children out in turn for a coke, ice cream, movie, shopping, or on a trip. (This is good for several weeks.)
2. Attend several of your child's functions this year (athletic contest in which the child participates, band, drama, etc.).
3. At one meal, at least, ask each child in turn how the day went for them. *Listen* to the answer.
4. Help a child with homework.
5. Watch cartoons with your small children on Saturday morning.
6. Teach your child how to jump rope, play jacks, catch, throw, and bat a ball, or ride a bike. Later, teach them how to drive a car, how to tie a necktie, polish shoes, put on makeup, coordinate colors in clothes, etc. Your covenant: I am willing to be my child's teacher until he/she tells me he would rather learn from someone else, or that he does not need my teaching.
7. I will take time once a week to put an arm around my child and say, "I'm glad you were born," or "You are handsome/pretty," or "You did a good job with that, and I am proud of you," or "I appreciate you for_____."
8. Be creative. Make up your own time covenant.

Train Up
a Child
14

It's a wonderful time to be alive. But many teenagers do not seem to know it. The second leading cause of death for teenagers in the United States is suicide. Some statistics suggest that suicide is probably the first cause of teenage deaths, because many suicides are done so they will look like accidents.

What's happening in the lives of teenagers that causes many to want to hit the ejection button? Dr. Marvin Trevitt, a psychiatrist who works with suicidal teenagers, outlined a few years ago some unnecessary pressures with which teenagers have a tough time coping.

Trevitt began his report by telling about Amy. Amy made her first "B" on her fifteenth birthday. Up to that point, it had been straight "A's" on everything.

When Amy got her first "B," she went straight home and hanged herself. Here's the note she left:

> Dear Mom and Dad: You have never said to me that I had to get good grades. As a matter of fact, we've hardly talked about it. But I know that you could not tolerate a failure. And if I fail in what I do, I fail in who I am. Goodbye, Amy.

Dr. Trevitt reported that we are dumping down our kids the philosophy that "happiness is what I do, not who I am."

Isn't it easy to make our children feel like our love is based upon their successful projects—grades, sports, performances, activities, etc.? When your child comes home with a grade lower than you think he ought to get, what kind of look do you have on your face?

When that little leaguer strikes out without even swinging the bat, or misses a pop fly that fell right into and *through* his glove, how do you react?

Do our children learn quickly that they are worth more if they do, do, do, and produce, produce, produce? Do they have to be at the top of the heap in our competitive world to be people of value?

Each child is valuable because of *who* he is, not because he is able to outdo the other children. It is a person's uniqueness that gives him self-worth. But *how* often do our children catch on to that?

The Bible teaches: "Train up a child in the way he should go, even when he is old he will not depart from it" (Proverbs 22:6). What does it mean to train up a child the way he should go? Rabbis tell us that there are two applications. The first one is the one we often miss. Rabbis stress the word "he." "Train up a child the way *he himself* should go." To train a child the way *he himself* is to go involves discovering, developing, and channeling his aptitudes. That takes time. For us to train up our children in the way they should go means that we need to know what each one is like. No two of them is alike. It would be wrong for us to expect one to be a copycat of the other. It is also wrong for us to program them to be like any other child. Each child is unique.

Isn't that true in your home? Do you know why? We are "God-ufactured" people, and God is a God of infinite variety. Of all the people in the world, no two have ever been exactly alike. Our fingerprint is one mark of our individualized uniqueness. As far as we can tell, there have never been two sets of fingerprints alike. Think how magnificent God is to be able to get that much variety into the little space of a fingertip. Just think what He can put into a five-foot tall person.

When a child is born, he gets half of a cell from his mother and half of a cell from his father. In each half cell is the potentiality of all the physical traits of his past heritage. That's variety. If someone in my past was seven feet tall, I had the potentiality of starring in basketball. But someone back there was about five and a half feet, so here I am standing short in the pulpit.

There are billions of different combinations that could come together when two half cells merge. That's why no two people will ever be totally identical.

Do you know what that means? That means you are valuable partly because you are unique (mostly because we are made in the

129

image of God). The most valuable things on planet earth are the rarest. Nobody is more rare than you and your children. (To say it another way, you are really odd—and so am I.)

To train up that unique child in the way *he himself* should go, means that we need to discover his interests, aptitudes, and abilities. That takes time!

I've known people who didn't like that understanding of Proverbs 22:6 at all. And I think one of the reasons is that it means we've got to invest *time* to know our kids. It means that I have no right to try to train up my son the way the boy down the road is going. When our second child was born about eighteen months after the first, I didn't know if I had enough love for the second one because I loved the first one so much. But isn't God fantastic! He always gives us enough love for each one.

Our second child was different from our first child, and that meant we had to let her have her uniqueness and individuality. Then we had to channel that uniqueness and individuality so they could get expressed and used. She'll not depart from that, for we're bringing out of her—her individuality, her personhood.

But it is so easy to compare our kids with other kids, and try to program them to do what we think they ought to do, and to be where we think they ought to be.

When Randy was in the fourth grade, and Rena was in the third grade, it happened. Before putting them to bed, we were reading the Bible together. I had Randy read. Then I had Rena read, and she read it as if she had written it herself. Perfecto! Inflections and everything just right. I turned to Randy and I said, "Randy, you're not reading as well as Rena." Mistake number one. Now, he wasn't reading poorly, just not as well as Rena. I could tell I was getting to him. "Aha! I've got him. Yippee!" So I decided to go ahead and give him a little psychological left uppercut. I said, "Now, Son, you cannot succeed at anything if you don't learn to read well." Mistake number two. Because, you see, he wasn't really interested in being a success at anything right then. He just wanted to climb a tree higher and throw a rock farther.

That's another mistake we make as parents. We often don't let our kids be ten-years-old for one whole year. We want to push them into adulthood, and then we wonder why they're getting into so much stuff we don't want them to get into about the time they're teenagers.

I could see I had Randy staggering psychologically. I had him on the ropes. So I decided to go ahead and give him the TKO. I said, "Son, when you come home from school tomorrow, no playing outside until you and I sit down and read. We're going to read together for one-half hour." He sniffed and said, "Okay, Dad." At that time in our lives we always tucked all of our kids in bed. In fact, not one of our kids would go to bed unless we tucked them in. That night, for some odd reason, Randy asked Mother to tuck him in, and I took the girls.

After Julia and I got the kids tucked in, we came back to the family room. A couple of minutes after we sat down, she said, "Buddy, (My nickname is Buddy. With a name like *Knofel* you cannot survive growing up unless you have a nickname.) do you remember how you liked to read when you were in the third or fourth grade?" I don't remember much about the third or fourth grade; I don't even remember my teachers' names. (Sorry about that, Teachers!) But I remembered an incident as if it had just happened, and I shared it with Julia.

Our principal, Lloyd Green, called all of the boys into his office and had us line up. That was *scary!* Then he said, "What I want you boys to do is to read a story over the sound system to everybody else." I hated to read. I can remember standing in that line behind Bobby Neil Young, the smartest kid in our class. And I can remember standing there thinking, "I wonder, if I grab my chest and yell, if Lloyd Green will let me out of this." Then I thought, "No, he wouldn't think I'm having a heart attack." Every step closer to the mike I tried to think of some scheme I could use to get out of it. The reason I remember that incident is because it was such a traumatic, negative experience for me.

Then Julia said, "That's interesting. Do you like to read now?" She knew I did, for I spend between seven and eight hundred dollars every year buying books. When you spend that much money buying books, you'd better say to your wife whether you read them or not, "Yeah, baby, I *love* to read!" Then she said, "Well how did you like the kids who didn't like to do anything but read back then?" I said, "I hated them. They just seemed like a bunch of sissies to me. They wouldn't make rubber guns and hit the girls with them, or any of the stuff like that." Then it dawned upon me what Julia was saying to me. I said, "I'm going to go talk to Randy."

I went down to his bedroom, and, sure enough, he wasn't asleep yet. In fact, he was sniffling. I knew I'd gotten to him. I sat on the edge of his bed, and I said, "Son, you know what? I've just been thinking." I did not say, "Son, your mother just zapped me between the eyes." I said, "Son, I've just been thinking that when I was your age, I just hated to read." He said, "Did you, Dad?" He came up and put his arms around me, and I put my arms around him, and I said. "Yes! And, Son, tomorrow you don't have to sit down and read. Change clothes, climb trees, throw rocks, and go to the creek."

You see, it's easy for us to compare one against the other. It's easy for us to want to yank one into adulthood when he's only ten years of age. I have the sneaking suspicion that if I had pulled off that dumb program with him, he might hate to read now, but he doesn't.

We need to help draw out and channel their uniqueness. If they have the interest and ability to be truck drivers, and we force them to be something else, I've got news for you. They won't like it. They may be constantly changing jobs and unhappy all their lives.

But there is another application for Proverbs 22:6. It is the moral way of God. Proverbs deals with it. There is a general way everybody is to go, and that is God's moral way.

We have often put "For Adults Only" across the pages of Proverbs. We really ought to put "For People Always, Regardless of Age." Take a look at the proverbs and learn from them what they say about child raising. For instance, in Proverbs 17:9 we read this, "He who covers a transgression seeks love, but he who repeats a matter separates intimate friends." That proverb will work no matter how old a person is. If we repeat a matter, we separate intimate friends.

I'll never forget when it happened. Rena came in and told us something Randy was doing that he shouldn't be doing. We called him in and disciplined him. About ten minutes later, Randy came in and told us something Rena should be doing that she was not doing. We called her in and disciplined her. Guess who's turn it was in about five minutes? Then Mother and I caught on. The name of the game was "tattletale." We made a new rule. Whoever tattles on the other to get him in trouble, gets the discipline. Do you know why that is a good rule? Because Proverbs will not fail: "He who repeats a matter separates intimate friends." We want our children to grow up not just being brothers and sisters, but also grow up being friends to one another. If your kids are tattling on each other, then you need to stop it. It is just the beginning of adult gossip.

"To show partiality in judgment is not good" (Proverbs 24:23). We are doing harm to a child when we blame others for his lack of achievement. For instance, rather than admit that another child's entry at the 4-H fair is better than our child's entry, we may either blame the judge or criticize the other entry. This can become an early lesson for our child not to accept the consequences for his actions, not to trust the honest appraisal of others, and not to respect the achievements of others. Such poor judgment prevents our child from learning to accept failure, and at the same time teaches him to rationalize a way out of difficulty.

"Ill-gotten gains do not profit" (10:2). This refers to advantages or goods obtained by illegal or underhanded means. Children can learn this very early through our reaction to their cheating in games or lessons. If we laugh at their cheating episodes, we are teaching them that such means are acceptable and advantageous. How they learn to play games will be reflected in their undertakings as adults. Cheating can help foster a life-style of selfishness and introvertism.

"Do not weary yourself to gain wealth" (23:4). This principle does not depreciate wealth, but rather it advises one against making wealth's acquisition his chief aim. Children develop their reasons for working from their parents' philosophy about working, and also from the ways parents motivate them to do their chores. Do they hear us complain about our jobs, and realize we remain at them only for the pay? Do we bribe them to do their work? Why do we approve or disapprove their choice of careers? What do they learn from us about being careful, thorough, and conscientious on the job?

One of society's desperate needs is for workers who take pride in the contribution their job makes toward their fellowmen. We need people on the assembly line who will do their best because a fellow human will be using the product. We need this philosophy, not only on the assembly line, but also in the administrative offices. Usually philosophy about work flows from the top down. Therefore, administrators cannot expect their workers to be really concerned about the finished product if the workers sense that the company is concerned about profit only.

Many people live a lifetime without feeling they have contributed to the well-being of others. What a tragic waste! What a difference the right philosophy of work would make, not only to the self-satisfaction of employers and employees, but also to the trust people would have in the products they purchase. It would make a difference even to the economy itself. Inflation could be reduced considerably if manufacturers did not have to build into their prices the cost of a high percentage of recalls and repairs under guarantee. What are company and union people doing to help develop a correct philosophy of work among us? What are parents doing?

Working for pay does not produce the satisfaction that working for people does. It is one thing to work for pay, but another to get paid for working. When we work just for pay, our work is mundane and often inferior, for our goal is reached every payday.

Recently we bought a new house built by men who worked for pay, without pride in the contribution their workmanship could make to the family who would live in the house. They were concerned only about getting the job done, so that another house could be started. The end product shows it. What a waste of workmanship! What a loss in contribution to a neighborhood and the comfortableness of families to come. I strongly suspect that most of these workmen learned in childhood this philosophy toward work. We need to teach our children about values. We can begin when they are little by letting them see what contribution their little chores make toward the well-being of the family.

Children usually enjoy working with their parents, but too often we are prone to say, "You're too young." When my son was four-years-old, he wanted to help me wash the car and change the oil. I let him, and he has never stopped enjoying doing it. I hope he never stops enjoying it. When he was seven, he wanted to help me mow the grass. I let him. I kept telling him how much fun it was, and that by keeping the lawn mowed we were helping to keep God's earth beautiful. Even our little daughter has the same philosophy about work. Where did she learn it? From him. She delights in helping her mother do the dishes, set the table, and bake cookies. If we do not teach and encourage children to fill some of their time with responsibilities, they will not know how to handle leisure time when they are older. Meaningless time breeds trouble in the land.

"He who conceals his transgressions will not prosper, but he who confesses and forsakes them will find compassion" (28:13). Are we helping our children follow this principle by having a home environment that helps them to be honest when they err? Do they experience our love regardless of their mistakes? Is their concept of acceptance "I love you if . . ."? If it is, they may become shackled to the expectations of others, and thus never develop their uniqueness.

A child needs parents in whom to confide when he really "blows it." If not, he will be uncomfortable with his parents. Failure to feel accepted by the closest family members when one has "goofed" may affect his ability to be honest with his mate when he marries. The parable of the prodigal son reveals what can happen when a child knows he can be honest with his parents.

"Correct your son, and he will give you comfort; he will also delight your soul" (29:17). God approves of spanking as an expression of love (13:24), "Dear Abby" notwithstanding. Children realize that discipline is a way that parents show their concern for behavior. A parent once said that her daughter remarked, "I'd hate to be Jane." When asked why, she replied, "She has never had a spanking. Her folks don't love her." Elementary teachers can easily spot the pupils who receive no discipline at home. Those children will do mischievous things, just to receive the discipline that reassures them someone does care about them. The progressive philosophy of child training (let the child decide for himself) has failed. Even some of its chief proponents have renounced it. God told us long ago that training a child demanded adult decisions rather than children's desires (22:6). A parent who does not discipline his child has set his heart upon the destruction of the child's personality (19:18). Children need parental guidance most when they want it the least.

Sometimes I think we love cherries more than children. We will drive stakes beside young cherry-tree sprouts to give them direction in growth, yet we are afraid we are interfering if we dictate standards for the direction of our children. Discipline is necessary. Though discipline with the rod is sometimes necessary, it is not to be the first and only kind of discipline. Children need various kinds, depending upon the situation. One of the worst things a parent can do, however, is to promise a spanking and then not give it. That is being dishonest with the child. It makes him wonder what you really do mean, and how you want him to act. It is one reason why many children lose respect for their parents. Parents should always fulfill their promises, so that the children will always believe them. Many children have learned that parents do not mean what they say unless their voices are raised in anger. How familiar is this scene:

Mother says, "It's time to pick up your toys, Honey."

Janie thinks, "I've got five minutes. She is in a good mood."

Mother says, more firmly, "Janie, please get your toys together."

Janie thinks, "I still have time."

Mother asks, "Janie, are you picking up your toys?"

Janie thinks, "Playtime is about over."

Mother says, loudly this time, "Janie, get those toys picked up!"

Janie thinks, "I can spin this top one last time."

Mother, with an angry voice, accompanied by heavy footsteps, "Janie, get busy!"

Janie begins picking up the toys.

Janie needs to know what Mother means when she says "Honey" in her calm, friendly voice. Janie will never know as long as Mother does not follow through with discipline at that first friendly, unheeded request.

Any discipline must be coupled with an explanation and followed up with acceptance. It is a good practice to say, "I am punishing you for . . . because I love you." The discipline itself should be executed in love, not anger. Discipline is to be done for a child's restraint and guidance, not for revenge and self-gratification of the parent.

There will be times when parents will make mistakes in discipline. We may discover that a child did not do the wrong we thought he did. When that happens, we must always admit our error, apologize, and ask for forgiveness. Once I pressed our five-year-old daughter into admitting a wrong I thought she had done; then I spanked her. Afterward I discovered she had not been guilty. After asking for her forgiveness, I pondered the question of why she had admitted doing something she had not done. Then it hit me! She had sensed that I did not believe her when she denied her guilt, so to fulfill my wishes, she admitted it. If a five-year-old will react like that when she feels she is not trusted, how would a teenager react if he felt his parents did not trust him? He will reason, "I might as well go ahead and do this wrong that my parents think I am doing. They won't believe me anyway." Children will try to live up to the trust or image we have of them. Let's give them something high to reach for!

At the same time, children will not be motivated to live up to your image of them if they do not respect you. Their respect for parents will be highest when the parents are living a sincere life of unselfish love. Their honest relationship with each other and with the children will determine the response. Respect can never be acquired by lavishing a person with things, but it will be acquired by living the principles of truth.

136

Satan knows several things about the significance of the parent-child relationship:

1. Parents are God-ordained custodians of the young. The best way to get children out of touch with God is to distract the parents from their primary responsibility as guardians.

2. The child's development depends largely upon parents' decisions. Satan will try to interfere with their unity of agreement.

3. The best time to fill people's hearts with folly is when they are young.

4. A team of at least three, mother, father, and God is necessary to rear a child properly. Satan will try his best to break up this team.

5. Bible teaching is the best curriculum for child training. Satan will seek to keep us too busy to share Scriptual truths with our children, lest we produce a generation of Timothys who are completely equipped for lives of righteousness (2 Timothy 3:14-17).

For Consideration or Discussion

Agree or Disagree:
1. American society teaches its children, "Happiness is what I do rather than who I am." Agree _____ Disagree _____ Discuss it.
2. Training a child the way he should go, is to train him the way *he himself* is to go. That is, help him discover, develop, and channel his aptitudes. Agree _____ Disagree _____ Discuss it.
3. If children go wrong, parents are usually responsible. Agree _____ Disagree _____ Discuss it.
4. If children have good moral examples in their parents, they require little verbal moral instruction. Agree _____ Disagree _____ Discuss it.
5. A solid and consistent Christian life in the parents is the best moral instruction children will ever have. Agree _____ Disagree _____ Discuss it.

Reflections:
1. Try to remember what adult taught you the most in your childhood about what it means to be a Christian.
2. Make your own "Book of Lists" on the various ways Christian parents can "train up a child in the way he should go." Share it with the class.

Bringing Up Teens

15

What do we owe our children anyway? My wife recently wrote an article for *Christian Standard* that discusses this question in a classical way. It was entitled "What We Owe Our Children."

> What our nation is doing to our children shocks, saddens, and concerns me. Child abuse and neglect escalate yearly; abortion has become a socially accepted solution to unwanted pregnancies. Runaway mothers have become as common as runaway fathers. More and more children are spending the greatest portion of their time in day-care centers or shifting for themselves in empty homes. And a majority of parents told Abigail VanBuren in a survey that if they had it to do over again, they would *not* have children. Our society is emphasizing that adults are going their own way to "find" themselves, while hardly anyone cares what happens to the children who are left behind.
>
> I know the job of parenting is difficult, frustrating, and not always exciting or fun. I am reminded of the time I was not able to leave the house for eight weeks straight because one or the other of our four children had the flu. As soon as one got well, another would say, "Mom, I'm sick." It got to the point that I thought I would scream if I had to change another bed or hear the word "Mommy" one more time. And as I was washing vomit out of the carpet for the fifth time, I asked myself, "What is a nice girl like you doing in a situation like this?" But neither can I forget the many happy and rewarding moments my

children have given me, and I cannot overlook what God has told me in His Word about what I owe them. Perhaps it would be helpful for you to be reminded also.

Life—God designed the process by which human beings would be formed. The man and woman are the vessels and the means for that life, but they do not create it. God makes clear in His Word that He gives the life that is the woman's womb (remember Sarah, Rebekah, Leah, Hannah, Elisabeth, etc.). . . .

He considers the fetus in the womb to be very precious. He made special provisions in His law for the protection of pregnant women (Exodus 21:22, 23) and condemned those who ripped open a woman with a child (Amos 1:13; 2 Kings 8:12). And He considers that life to be a person from the moment of conception. When He told Mary of Elisabeth's conception (Luke 1:36), He said she had conceived a *son*—not a thing, a cell, or a blob. When referring to Rebekah's pregnancy, the Scripture speaks of *children* struggling within her and two *nations* and *peoples* being in her womb. They could hardly be considered non-entities. God told Jeremiah that He formed him in his mother's womb and set him apart to be a prophet before he was born (Jeremiah 1:5).Would he declare anything less than a person to be a prophet?

God gives us children as gifts, as rewards, as prizes. He considers them to be valuable parts of the family, signs of a secure, successful family, and are to be the sources of our pride (Psalm 127:3-5; 128:3, 4; 144:12-15). How can we then dare to usurp the authority and the will of God by taking the life of a child through abortion or child abuse? How can we then dare to throw away these precious gifts from God as if they were just so much garbage? We must allow them to live out their lives. Only God has the right to decide when they should die.

Love—God directs us to love *agape*-style in every human relationship we have. This love includes our children. Such love means a total giving of ourselves; it is acting for the benefit of our children, not for ourselves. When Paul spoke of his love for the Corinthians and how he thought of them as his children, he expressed the results of this type of love: "I will most gladly spend and be expended for your souls" (2 Corinthians 12:15, *New American Standard Bible*). According to the Greek, he was saying, "I am willing to be consumed, to be completely spent out for your benefit." He was willing to give his all, not grudgingly, in irritation or frustration, but *gladly*.

Of course, this type of love does not happen overnight or magically when the newborn infant is placed in the parents' arms. It involves a great deal of effort and patience. It involves living out in daily life all the aspects of *agape*-love that are listed in 1 Corinthians 13:4-7.

However, giving this type of love does not mean we become slaves to our children, that we give them all that they desire, or that we love them to the exclusion of all others. It is a balanced love, a love that will benefit them, a love that means we place our children in high priority but not a priority that supersedes our responsibilities to our mates or to God.

With this love, we will not neglect our children. We will not go off in our own way and let them essentially shift for themselves. We will seek to provide them with a stable home and with parents who love each other. We will not think of them or treat them as intrusions but as blessings, not as restrictions but as rewards. We will give of ourselves which means giving them *quantity* time. We will listen to them, comfort them, praise them, motivate them, clean up after them, help them with their homework, go to their school events and sports activities with them, play with them, laugh with them, weep with them, and simply "be there" when they need us.

Light—God has entrusted children to us so that we might enlighten them so they will grow to Christian maturity. We are to "light" the way for them with instruction, guidance, and discipline. We are to educate our children in God's wisdom, and His wisdom comes from His Word (2 Timothy 3:14, 15).

But how do we get God's Word into the hearts and minds of our children? We teach our children mostly by our own examples in daily living. God expects us as parents to live life before the eyes and ears of our children with His life-style and viewpoint, not the world's (Deuteronomy 4:9, 10; 11:18-21). But we must realize that we cannot play-act and get away with it. Our children can see right through the masks we wear.

If we say prayer is important but our children never see or hear us pray, they will follow our examples rather than our words. If we say the Bible is an important guide to our living but we never read it, the children will follow our examples rather than our words. If we say Bible school and worship on Sunday are important but don't go if another activity interferes, our children will follow our examples rather than our words. If we say God's way is the right way but we hardly give God a thought as we go about our daily lives, our children will follow our examples rather than our words.

But being good examples is not all there is to it. We must not kid ourselves into thinking that as long as we read the Bible to our children, take them to church services, and live committed, moral lives that our children will grow up to be fine Christian adults. We must also guide and correct them. Children cannot be left to determine their own way, for they are selfish, foolish individuals. Left to their own devices, children will destroy themselves and all those who touch their lives. They need correction in order to learn to relate to others unselfishly. (See Proverbs 15:10; 19:18, 20; 22:15; 23:13, 14; 29:15, 17.)

To God, discipline is a very important matter and not to be taken lightly. It is not to be administered impulsively but only after careful thought about the individual child and the situation. Discipline should come from love and be a natural part of a family relationship. It is difficult and inconvenient to take the time and effort to administer discipline appropriately, but the result of children being guided to live in God's way makes it well worth it (Hebrews 12:5-11 describes how God administers discipline and His thoughts about it).

Although Proverbs makes clear that physical punishment is a part of discipline in God's view, we also know from other Scriptures that God would never condone

141

physical abuse, harsh or unjust punishment, belittling, or treating children as things or pieces of property. Love and caring must be the basis (Ephesians 6:1-4).

Liberty—Our children are individuals with minds and wills; they are not puppets whose strings we can pull or lumps of clay that we can mold. In their later teens, they will come to a point when they will need to handle life in their own way. And as much as it will hurt us, we must give them the freedom to make mistakes. They may fall flat on their faces; they may do things we do not agree with. But if we insist on always supervising their every move, on making all their decisions for them, or on plotting every step of their journey through life, they will not mature properly. They will not find their own value-systems or establish their own relationship to God.

Keeping our youth locked up in a box will only retard their development into adulthood. We do not want our parenthood to entrap our youth like flypaper, causing them to lose their motivation, their spirit, their individuality, and their creativity. We can learn from the story of the Prodigal Son (Luke 15:11-32). The son wanted to go his own way; he wanted to live life on his own terms. The father gave him that freedom, and the son made mistakes. But through his experience, he realized what his priorities in life should be.

It's not easy to bring up children through teen years in these days. (Has it ever been easy?)

I will never forget how I felt. It was one of the most uneasy feelings I had ever had. I was away from home on a speaking trip when our son had his thirteenth birthday. I did not know whether to go back home or not. I had heard so much about the terrible teens, and we'd never had a teenager in our house before. I thought when I was away from home on his thirteenth birthday, "This will be the last day of peace I will have in my whole life." I thought when I got back home everything would be different. He would be one big rebellion, ready to find something else to complain about. But when I got home life didn't cave in at all.

Bringing up teenagers does not have to be the negative, knock down, drag out that a lot of people seem to think is inevitable.

142

Bringing up teenagers doesn't happen the day a boy or girl has the thirteenth birthday. No, no. Bringing up teenagers begins whenever a mother and a father realize they are going to have a new baby. Bringing up teenagers begins with the priorities the parents begin to set or realign when they realize one made in the image of God is going to grace their family.

Bringing up teenagers gets into full gear the day that baby is born. And it continues through every stage of the child's development, until he gets to be a teen and then through his teen days.

Up until the time a child hits the teen years, he goes through five stages, including his teenage stage. They are stages of life, and every stage of life is like a "Y." We're going to look at this "Y." In fact, you could just about call the "Y," "Youth in Development." Every stage is a stage of *discovery*. There are certain new things a person discovers in every stage of life; a child begins to specialize in relating to certain things in certain ways.

Every stage in life is a *turning point* for a person. He comes to a turning point very much like we come to a "Y" in a road. What happens at this stage conditions which way he may go when he is an adolescent or an adult. It may *condition* which way he goes, but it does not always *determine* it. We are not people who are determined. No, we are people of choice. We are people who can change their minds and change their directions. If that were not possible, then conversion would not be possible. What happens in our formative days conditions which way we may go later in life.

Infancy

Stage number one is the stage of infancy. We could say the stage of infancy is from birth to two years of age, but that is unrealistic because people are different. Sometimes certain aspects of the stage of infancy go on until somebody is three or four or five.

The stage of infancy is a stage during which the infant is discovering *others* and learning to relate to others. What happens in this stage can affect him later on in his life—whether he trusts others or goes the negative way and mistrusts others. What he needs more than anything else in his infancy stage is a good association with others. The primary need a little baby has is to be accepted, to be touched, to be talked to, to be loved, to be held close. As that kind of experience grows, he learns he can trust other people.

The most important person during these days is his mother. It is wrong for mothers to think, "Well, after we have a baby, I'll go back to work in a couple of months and leave the baby with somebody else. Then when the baby gets older, and can talk and needs me, I'll come home." No! The first major need of a baby is for the mother to be there. Many primitive cultures have learned that, and many times the babies develop faster than our babies in America. This happens primarily because of the relationships that mothers know they are to give to their children. It is the quality of a mother's relationship that really conditions the amount of trust that is planted in a child during this infancy stage.

It is also important during this infancy stage not to have a set of "dos" and "don'ts" without explanation. When you say, "No!" to a child who reaches out for something at eight or nine or ten months, don't just say "No!" and slap his hand. Sit down and explain *why*. The child is not going to be able to speak back what you explain, but the child is going to sense that you take him seriously. You love him; you have a reason for this. So back up your "dos" and "don'ts" with a system of positive communication.

Early Childhood

The second stage is the stage of early childhood. In this stage the child is beginning to discover and relate to *himself*. What happens in this stage as he discovers himself and starts relating to himself is very important. In this stage he learns to be a person who can cooperate or be totally autonomous, totally turned into himself.

This is the stage that many people call the "terrible twos." The child discovers that he has fingers that move out there, and those fingers are attached to this arm, and this arm is attached to this shoulder, and that is *mine!* And these fingers are *mine!* And this body is *mine.* In fact, it is during this stage that he also learns to say the words, "Mine, Me," and he knows what they mean. He knows toys are "mine," and, even if they're not his, he wants them to be his. He can make that differentiation.

He discovers that he is in this world with others, and he starts pushing himself. It is during this stage that he is really raising the question in his mind, "Okay, I've discovered other people and now I'm discovering myself. What I want to know is this: Who's boss around here anyway?" Every child goes through this period of time, and it can cause the mother to pull out her hair.

It is this time they want to be loved by the others. This is the stage of real inconsistency. Do you remember some of the inconsistencies? One time during the "terrible twos," a child may snuggle up

144

close to you and say, "Mommy, I love you." Three seconds later, "I hate you." During this time when they are learning that they have muscles they can control, the inconsistency is seen in such things as holding their toys tightly. Because they're in control, they don't want to give them to anybody else. They don't want their playmates to take their toy. But the inconsistency is seen when you are riding along in the car. Suddenly out the open window goes a toy. All is part of their learning to be in control. "I'll hold on to things; that is my decision and my control. I'll let go of something anytime I want to let go of something."

It is during this stage that a child can go into a temper tantrum. A tempter tantrum is their attempt to force the issue, "I am in control." Do you know what makes a temper tantrum work? It is whenever they get their way because of one. I tell you, kids are smart. They remember that the temper tantrum worked, and their little insides are saying, "Ha! Ha! Ha! I've got her. She's on the run. If it worked once, it will work again." And the first time you let a temper tantrum work, you have set your child on a pattern. Your child is getting more and more comfortable with being in control.

This is a time when children will also want to evade other people and hide. It is a period of time when you have to be firm, and you have to be consistent in the child's discipline. The first time the child looks at you as if to say, "I'm going to get you," you need to stop that. Whenever the child hits back during discipline, you must get that under control also.

During the "terrible twos," they want to do things they cannot do. Praise them for what they can do. Tell them, "You're growing up. You're growing up. I love you." And when you discipline them, be sure to back it up with, "I love you and I care. You're special, and you are worth something."

Don't work at changing too much too early, such as potty training. Don't get the idea if your child is not potty trained by two, "I've got a dumb, retarded kid on my hands." People are different. Muscle control is different. Don't let that bug you.

Middle Childhood

The third stage is an interesting stage. I just call it the stage of middle childhood. This is the stage when our kids are learning and discovering *opportunities*. Everything around them is an opportunity. It is the stage of multiplying imagination. They like to experiment with this and that. It is the stage of the *"go-aholic."* Remember that? They are into this and out of it. They want to try everything. They want to open doors when they are not old enough to open doors; they want to paint the house when they are not old enough to paint the house. Everything is an opportunity. A whole world of opportunities is opening up.

They want to try baseball; they want to try football; they want to try wrestling. It's an exciting stage for them. They dream about the future. They dream about being heroes. It is the stage of an ongoing, initiating spirit. It is a stage where they enter into the competitive world, and they think they can do everything. They like games of competition. They like to try!

But you know something? They don't like to finish a thing! That can really get to parents. They may want to start helping with the dishes, but they get two wipes in and leave. You give them tasks and they go unfinished. That just blows your mind. But remember, they are interested in opportunities, a touch-and-go world, a try-it-and-leave-it world. In this stage, everything is like being in an ice cream factory, and they can taste it all. It is very important to allow them to experiment without destroying, and to understand that they are not going to finish very many tasks.

This is the stage also where they don't mind failures. It is a stage where they may start playing football and not do very well. And you know what? They will forget it and go on to something else. If one of their playmates makes them very mad, because they didn't get to do something with a toy or a game, they can come home and say, "I'm never going to play with that kid again." Guess what happens? Four mintues later they're on the phone; they want to play a game. They forget easily. Why do they forget easily? Because it is a new opportunity. It is a new world out there, and they want to get on with something different.

At this particular stage the child is being conditioned to be flexible or inflexible later on in his life. If you handle him in a negative way, and don't let him experiment, and don't let him do anything because it is going to dirty the house, he'll end up being more paralyzed and fixated. A lot of parents make this mistake, because they think house cleanliness is more important than children's experimentation with some opportunities. They will not let the child even help with cookies because they mess up the kitchen. What is more important than the child seeing a world of opportunities?

It is important to relate to the child in a way that his initiating spirit, his creativity, is not destroyed. At the same time, the child

146

does not go unchecked. You cannot let him go wild. If you do, you will produce a hypertensive, "go-aholic" person, who always has his human accelerator down to the floor. It is full speed ahead even when he is at the rest stops. He never settles down. He moves from project to project—may never get anything done.

But you can kill his initiative by saying, "You're too dumb; you're too small; you can't try that." He may grow up into the teen years feeling that his inner capacities are not as good as another's inner capacities. He begins to feel a low self-esteem: "I cannot do things; I cannot make decisions on my own." If that is the way he grows up, when he gets to be a teenager, he will not be free and flexible. The chances are very high that he will allow the group and the gang to make decisions for him. He doesn't feel like he can make any decisions, because you've never let him make any. You've never let him experiment at home.

Late Childhood

The next stage is late childhood. At this stage, children discover that *jobs can get finished,* not just begun. This is the stage where they slow down from a touch and go. They are not just experimenting with everything all at the same time. They begin to be fulfilled, not by just starting things, but also by finishing some jobs.

It is very important at this stage that we relate to them in such a way they can finish a job and feel fulfillment. But the toughest obstacle in letting a child finish a job is our impatience. We often want them to hurry up becaue they take too much time. We fail to understand we are bringing up teenagers and that takes time.

Another reason this is a hard stage for parents is because children do not do their jobs the way we would do them.

Folks, they are little tots and we can't expect them to do them the way we do. So we have to allow them to do things in a way which is not quite as superior as ours. (It might be messy, and it might make us want to pull our hair out.)

A story has been told about a man who had a child at this stage. He called his parents' home, and the mother answered. He said, "Mom, I want to talk to Dad." Dad got on the phone, and he said, "Dad, I just called to tell you, 'I'm sorry,' " The dad said, "What do you mean, 'You're sorry'?" The son said, "Well, my son is helping me put tile down in our bathroom, and I remembered all the times I helped you. I'm just calling to tell you I am sorry."

Adolescent

The stage is the teenage stage. You know what's going on in the teenage stage? The teenagers are discovering *society at large,* the whole society. What happens in this stage is that teenagers are going through every one of the other stages all over again. They are discovering other people, particularly the opposite sex, and other adults besides those at home, and they are learning to trust or mistrust them. They are discovering things about themselves they never knew. Their bodies are changing physically, and they are changing emotionally. They are discovering tasks that are teenage oriented.

They are discovering new opportunities—like driving a car, going on a date, going to the ball game without mother and dad. This is the stage where all of society has focused in on them, and it is a stage where they are very, very vulnerable.

Since they are changing very rapidly, they get pimples, their voices change; they get hurt very easily. They get hurt if they're not asked to a dance; they get hurt if they are not asked to a birthday party. It is a stage of confusion for them. Many times parents tell them to act like adults, but they're not allowed to be one and they know it. So they look for heroes to trust in.

It is a stage where he begins to be a bit autonomous—he is breaking away from mother and dad. He is beginning to ask the question, just like the "terrible twos," "Who's boss around here?" That one question can raise a lot of problems unless it was settled many, many years ago. The biggest tension with teenagers is that they are changing.

Parents must understand, "I have to do some changing with the teenager." I cannot treat him as a terrible two. I cannot treat him as a child. He is growing into adulthood, and he has a lot of decisions, a lot of choices." We have to gradually begin to give him freedom. A teenager is going to move into the age where he is going to make decisions on his own. If we don't help him to do that by giving him some freedom, by letting him go with our hands open, by holding him close and at the same time letting him have freedom, then, as soon as he leaves the house, we may be shocked at the kind of decisions he will make. We've not given him the kind of family fellowship that he needs.

Bringing up teenagers can be a tremendous delight, or it can be drudgery. It doesn't start when they have their birthdays. It starts on the day you know one is coming. If you have made mistakes in the past, and they hit the teenage years, now is the time to sit down and admit to them, "I've made some mistakes. I want to share some of them with you." Because teenagers are not determined, they can change into the kinds of people God wants them to be, regardless of how much you might have goofed. God's grace is always greater than man's circumstances.

For Consideration or Discussion

Not many teenagers can tell adults how they really feel, but if they could, they might say:

I am an early teen. I am terribly embarrassed about myself. I feel awkward. My hands and feet don't do what I tell them. I lack confidence in myself. I don't know how to carry on a conversation, especially with new acquaintances; adults, and the opposite sex. I don't like the way I look.

I am a midteen. I am only a little awkward. It is difficult to be a Christian these days. I get lots of pressure from my peers to experiment with drugs or to be sexually active. I am aware of my sexuality, and that is very interesting—and sometimes quite troubling. The competition is tough in everything: to make good grades, to make the team, to be popular.

I am a late teen. I have done a few things that do not make me proud. I still don't have much self-confidence. I am anxious about my future. I am having trouble choosing a career. My heart has been broken a time or two. My parents don't realize I'm grown up. They keep giving me advice I don't want to hear, and they treat me like a child. I want to leave home, and yet it's scary to be on my own. My religious ideas are changing, and that sometimes confuses me. My friends are scattering to work and college. Often I think everything is changing.

If you are a teen, and if the feelings described above are accurate, discuss them with the group. Perhaps you can add to them.

If you are an adult, discuss how adults might be helpful to early, mid, and late teens.

149

Teaching Children About Sex

16

I remember being told in ministry class in college, "Never teach about sex. If you do, people will think you are interested in it."

People *are* interested in sex. The church should teach what the Bible says about it, and parents should teach their children about it. But neither the church nor the home has been noted for its up-front contribution. Consequently, our children have learned too much from outside both the church and home. Often all they hear or see comes from the perverted worldly view of sex.

The home is the natural place for education about sex. Parents should take advantage of those moments when children ask their questions. When children become inquisitive about the physical side of sex, parents need to answer them honestly. *How* we answer them may mold their concept about sex as much as *what* we say. If we act shocked at their questions, we communicate to them that sex is dirty and something to be ashamed of. If we give them a complicated lecture, we communicate that sex is complex and boring. If we answer them clearly and honestly, we communicate that sex is another natural part of God's design for life within marriage.

Julia and I have never been dishonest when our children asked questions. For instance, when they asked, "What is that Daddy?" we never made up some answer; we called it a penis. (However, we didn't volunteer to name certain parts at the same time we were teaching them to touch and name eye, nose, ear, etc.)

Children ask questions at an early age, but they do not always want all the details. Randy and Rena were four and five when Julia was pregnant with Rhonda. Julia let them feel the baby's movement. They once asked, "How did the baby get in there?" At four and five they were not wanting details. Julia simply answered,

"When two people love each other, God makes it possible for a baby to be formed in a mother." When they asked, "How will the baby come out?" Julia said. "When it's time, your Daddy will take me to the hospital and the doctor will help us. He knows exactly what to do." Her answers satisfied them.

Had we been telling them all along that a stork brought them to us, it might have been tough to convince them that they had as much worth as a baby not delivered by some bird. We kept assuring them that the process and development of Rhonda was just exactly the way it had been with them.

When Julia was pregnant with Rachel, Randy was ten-years-old. At that age when he wanted to know "How did the baby get in there?" he wanted to know *how*. And don't think that ten-year-olds of today are dumb about that sort of thing. If you try to snow them, you are just fooling yourself. You aren't fooling them one bit. There is enough drawn on most public restroom walls to advance our children years beyond where some of us were at that age.

When Randy asked that question of his mother while I was away on a trip, she sat down with him and discussed the reproductive function of the male penis and female vagina. She explained that the male penis penetrates the vagina, the man's sperm finds an egg in the woman, and a baby begins. But she also talked with him about how this activity is to be done by married couples. It was a beautiful time to teach our developing son about morals in sex.

When Randy was thirteen years old, I decided to have a father/son talk with him. No one had ever done anything like that with me, so quite frankly, I was uncomfortable. I suspect many fathers have put such a talk off because of the same uncomfortable feeling. In order to help other fathers, I have decided to outline what I talked over with Randy:

1. *The changes in the body.* I discussed that soon his voice would start changing, hair would appear under his arms, around his penis, and on his face. These are signs that he is becoming more of a man.

2. *Erection.* I told him that he would wake up many mornings with an erection (too late, Dad, it had already been happening). I explained that an erection was one way to help control the bladder. But the ability to have an erection meant that he was approaching the time when he could get a girl pregnant. I discussed the manufacturing of semen in his body and the reality of wet dreams. I reviewed how a girl gets pregnant.

3. *The difference between boys and girls.* I discussed that boys are stimulated by touch and sight. That didn't mean he was a dirty old man. God made boys that way. But I also explained that girls are not stimulated by touch and sight as much as boys. Because girls are not stimulated this way, many times they encourage boys to look and touch. I encouraged him not to hang around with loose girls. I encouraged him to be friendly with everyone! However, he must be the one to decide who his close friends are.

I explained to him that many girls have become pregnant who said, "I'm not that kind of girl." But every girl is that kind of girl. A girl's head says, "No, I won't go all the way" when petting starts. But God has made her body in such a way that if she allows it to continue changes begin to go on inside her body. Eventually her mind is still saying, "No," but her body starts saying, "Hmmm." Her mind still says "No," but her body begins to say, "Well, maybe." Her mind still says, "No," when her body says, "I think so." And when her body says, "Yes, yes," her mind is not in control. Every girl needs to know that about her body—and so do the boys.

4. *Sexual purity until marriage.* I talked with Randy about being a virgin until marriage.

5. *Masturbation.* I discussed what masturbation is. I told him that many stories about masturbation are wrong—such as masturbation will destroy the brain. But I also told him that a boy can make such a habit of masturbation that it does affect his thinking. Too much masturbation can lessen the enjoyment of sex within marriage.

While I did not say "never masturbate," I did say, "Son, if you ever discover that you are doing this very often, will you come to me so we can talk about it.?"

6. *Homosexuality.* I discussed what this is. I told him what to look out for in homosexual approaches. I stressed being careful in public restrooms. I also stressed coming to his parents any time he was approached in any homosexual way.

7. *VD.* We discussed various kinds of VD, and how it is becoming an epidemic, and how it is controlled.

Here is an outline about VD:

VD stands for veneral disease. It can be a very serious infection contracted by having intercourse with someone with the disease. There is no way to tell whether or not the other person has the disease. Many times the other person does not even know it. It is passed from person to person, and it is in an epidemic stage in many parts of this country. There are several kinds of VD. Two of the most common are gonorrhea and syphilis.

Gonorrhea. Occasionally gonorrhea may attack the membranes of the eye, resulting in blindness. An infected mother can cause her baby to be born blind.

The first symptoms of gonorrhea usually appear within a week after contact, but they can take as long as three weeks. With men the inflamation usually causes a powerful, burning sensation during the urination. The infected penis discharges a whitish fluid or pus. If not treated, it can spread to other members of the body.

A woman with gonorrhea may feel no pain and notice no early symptoms. That's why she may not know she is a carrier. However, she may have some pain in the lower abdomen. The infection can spread so in the woman that she becomes sterile. It can spread to the bladder, kidneys, rectum, and even cause meningitis and death.

Syphilis. This is a tricky disease. It often appears cured, but it can go through stages—primary, secondary, and _____ . The infection spreads throughout the body within a week.

The first sign of primary infection is a painless sore that may resemble a blister anytime from nine days to three months after contact. It usually appears on the head of the penis in men and on the labia in women. It may disappear in ten to forty days after treatment, making the person think it is cured when it isn't. If mouth sores are present, syphilis may be passed on by kissing.

Two to six months after the sore disappears, the secondary stage may begin. It may last up to two years. The first symptom of the second stage is usually a rash that may appear on any part of the body and spread. It doesn't itch, and it looks something like measles. This rash is often accompanied by headaches, fever, and a general feeling of illness. Hair may fall out; bones and joints can become painful.

The third stage may remain hidden for fifteen years or more. A blood test won't reveal the presence of it. This final stage can be fatal. It affects the central nervous system and heart. It can damage any organ of the body.

There are many other kinds of VD. Some new strains have emerged with the rise of homosexual activity and anal sex. Some of these new strains do not have any known cure.

It is essential that our young people be counseled to remain virgins until marriage. Individual lives, mates, and future babies can be affected by VD.

8. *Pornography.* I discussed what pornography is. I discussed the danger to a person's emotions, and the lack of appreciation of the opposite sex that pornography communicates. I am not naive enough to think that a growing boy will not look at a magazine with naked women. If you think that, your head is really in the sand. However, a boy can have problems which are difficult to overcome if he becomes obsessed by that. So Randy and I have the understanding that he will come to me if he wants to spend very much time looking at any form of pornography.

I would encourage fathers to discuss at least the above minimum outline with their sons.

Mothers should talk with their daughters about breast changes and care, the start of the menstrual period, its significance and care.

Talks with our children should include Paul's advice in at least two places. Read 1 Corinthians 6:15-20 and 1 Thessalonians 4:3-8.

For Consideration and Discussion

Do you realize?:
1. That you begin to teach children about sex the moment the child is born, for your own sexual attitudes will be communicated to the child throughout the rearing years.
2. That the way you interact with your spouse teaches your child about sex. If you treat your spouse with respect and tenderness and responsibility, you are modeling the relational behavior which is the foundation of a positive and responsible attitude toward sex. The healthiest attitude toward sex is a healthy attitude toward the opposite sex. As a matter of fact, "sex" is an abstraction. There is no such thing as "sex." There is only the opposite sex and a relationship with an actual person, a human being of the opposite sex. What we call "sex" is a relationship with such a person. Therefore, your relationships with your spouse is the most profound sex education for your child.

Do you know?:
1. The basic information on human sexuality? Does it include a basic outline of sexual/genital anatomy, together with the proper names for the various parts of the human reproduction system. If you don't, how can you explain this to your child in an *accurate* and *competent* and *comfortable* manner?

For books on human sexuality, see the list at the end of Chapter 12 (Sex and Spirituality).

A Word
to the Children
17

Children have difficulty understanding why they must obey their parents. Scripture is specific on this responsibility: "Children, obey your parents in the Lord, for this is right" (Ephesians 6:1). In Ephesians, Paul outlines the eternal plan of God which is to unite all things (1:1-14). Such unity was made possible through the sacrifice of Jesus. Because of Him, oneness can be achieved among people, despite their differences (2:11-22). Within the church that unity is to be demonstrated (3:10). Paul enjoins all Christians to live in that unity (4:1-16). He further outlines some of the attitudes that will maintain unity (4:25—5:21).

Since it is God's purpose to unite all, it is the devil's purpose to work toward disunity. He is looking for an opportunity to cut into unity (4:27). When he succeeds, the Spirit of God is grieved (4:30). If we do not manifest the characteristics that can foster unity, and if we do not put away bitterness, wrath, clamor, and slander (4:31), we oppose God's plan (1:10). We give opportunity to the devil (4:27), and we grieve the Holy Spirit (4:30).

Immediately after developing God's plan for initiating and maintaining unity, Paul begins to outline the responsibilities of people in the home (5:22—6:4). Why? The answer is clear: If husbands are not loving their wives, if wives are not submitting to their husbands, if children are not obeying parents, and if parents are provoking children to wrath, there will be disunity in the home. It is impossible to have unity in the church, if there is disunity in the homes.

Children who do not obey their parents introduce disunity into the home and the church. They act in opposition to God's plan, give opportunity to the devil, and grieve the Holy Spirit. This is serious! Children who fail to obey parents, rebel against God's will.

155

Failing to obey parents is also rebelling against one's own well-being. That is why Paul adds, "That it may be well with you, and that you may live long upon the earth" (6:3). What does obedience to parents have to do with personal well-being? Alienation in family relationships affects the total person. It affects both physical and psychological health. A person is not at ease with himself when living amidst alienation. It affects sociological health. A person who cannot obey his parents has a difficult time relating well to any authority in society. Thus school and career days are affected. A person's role in marriage will be affected. The capacity to submit to a marital mate is lessened when a person has not been able to submit to parents. Selfishness becomes a life-style. Alienation affects spiritual health. Our relationship to God cannot be divorced from our relationship to parents, for it is His will that children obey them. Our relationship to Christ cannot be complete, for His example was to be subject to Mary and Joseph (Luke 2:51).

Unwillingness to obey parents brings insecurity to both the children and the parents. Parents need the loving response of their children. Children's relationships with their parents help meet some of their basic needs.

The father has a need to express authority; he needs the child's respect for him as leader of the family. In loving him, the child should give him cooperation and the luxury of making mistakes. After all, doesn't he make allowances for your mistakes? If a child does not respect his father and obey him, the father's leadership growth will lessen and he may become insecure in his headship role.

The mother has a basic need to express tenderness, care, and peacemaking. If a child does not allow his mother this expression, her feminity will lessen and her insecurity will mount. Since a woman tends to take things personally, a child cannot rebel without deeply hurting his mother. She needs the words "I love you" from her children. She also has a part in "having dominion," for both male and female were given the ability to have dominion (Genesis 1:28). The mother best expresses her dominion over the things of household management (Proverbs 31:10ff.) But if her desire to express love to her children is blocked, she may fill that vacuum by trying to dominate both her children and husband. Thus, a child's failure to obey may be a major factor in the blurring of roles. This causes a serious identity crisis among youth.

If they do not see how the male is meant to function at home,

156

and how the female is meant to function, young people can become confused about their own roles. On the one hand, they may not like what they see in their sex role as observed in their mother or father. They may then decide to adopt the characteristics of the other sex. On the other hand, not liking what they see in the other sex role as observed at home, they may decide to have intimate relations with only their own sex, thus creating homosexuality. No wonder Paul wrote, "Obey your parents; for this is right."

Young people, don't bring insecurity to your parents. When you are out later than usual without phoning your parents, they will spend a sleepless night. Why? Because they love you. Is that a crime? You need to consider the kind of society in which we are living. Every day girls are abused, raped, and murdered. Every day boys are killed or permanently injured by auto accidents. Your parents have no way of knowing you are safe when you are out beyond curfew, unless you call them. Be fair. Take away their anxiety. Show them the consideration and love that you expect from them. Call them!

Now! How do you get along with your brothers and sisters? Be a friend to them by setting a good example for them. If you think that familiarity breeds contempt, that you cannot be close friends with your siblings because you live with them and know them too well, what makes you think you can be a part of a happy marriage later? You will be living with that mate and will know him or her well. Try to treat your brothers and sisters at least as well as you treat company.

Try to bring into your homelife the characteristics of God as outlined in 1 Corinthians 13. As a son or daughter, as a brother or sister, be kind and patient. Don't be arrogant, or demand your own way. Rejoice in the good of your family members. This kind of life is not for adults only, but for Christians always.

As a young person, you are not just the church of tomorrow. You are also part of the church today. You can help the family of God have the life-style needed in the church as you live your life according to God's will and for God's role for you in the home. God knows better than you do the way you should go. He knows your development demands the authority of your parents. If this were not His intention, He would have given other instructions. Evidently we all need the instructions He gave. If they are not followed, our healthy adjustment will be greatly hampered.

I can just hear you saying, "But my folks don't understand me!"

157

This is doubtful. But if it is so, how about you? Do you do unto others as you want them to do unto you? Do you try to understand your parents? Do you listen? Do you pray for them by name? Do you live to help meet their needs, wants, and desires?

Do not demand to be the center of attention. A secure family rests largely upon the fact that the mother and father can cleave to each other. If you give your mother the freedom to allow your father to be her center of attention, and give your father the freedom to allow your mother to be his center of attention, your needs will be met. Never act in such a way as to pit them against each other. Too many children play this game. Little do they realize that they weaken the cleaving relationship between the mother and father. They lessen the security of the home, and with it their own security.

For Consideration or Discussion

For children only:

Read Colossians 3:12-14. Test it for six weeks by:

1. Obeying your parents without protest, even when you disagree with them. (Certain unusual situations might be expected, such as a command from your parent that you steal something.)
2. Asking your parents what you could do to be helpful *before* they ask you for your help.
3. Doing some household chores you know your parents would like you to do without being asked.
4. Note or personal word expressing appreciation to your parents for all they have done for you.
5. Bringing your mom or dad a surprise, inexpensive gift—a flower, something you made with your hands, or *volunteer* to baby-sit so that your parents may have a night out.
6. Checking your tendency to argue *every* time your parents ask you to complete a chore.
7. Doing your homework on time, without being asked.
8. When you have done these things, thank God if you have seen improvement in your relationship with your parents. If you have seen no improvement, take satisfaction in the growth you have experienced while obeying the Lord.

Divorce and Remarriage

18

Divorce is not a modern-day invention. It is as ancient as Moses. And not only nonchurch people experience divorce. Just watch all those hands go up in any group of Christians when you ask, "How many of you have experienced a divorce yourself or in your immediate family (parents, children, brothers, or sisters)?"

Indeed, divorce is one of the major issues in our society. No wonder people in the church are asking questions. Just where does divorce place a person in his relationship to God, to his church, to eternity, etc.? The questions become more urgent when remarriage is being considered. This is probably the toughest practical problem facing the church today.

Just what does the Bible teach about divorce?

The Old Testament and Divorce

After quoting Genesis 2:24, Jesus concluded that the verse taught that God's original intention was for two people to remain married until separated by natural death. "Consequently they are no longer two, but one flesh. What therefore God has joined together, let no man separate" (Matthew 19:6). He made it clear that divorce was not a part of God's original intention for marriages. "Because of your hardness of heart, Moses permitted you to divorce your wives; but from the beginning it has not been this way" (Matthew 19:8).

However, sin entered the world, and sin changed things. God does not like what sin does, but He works with the situation for the good of mankind. Although God's original intention was for marriage to continue until natural death, He allowed two other ways for a marriage to be dissolved. One way was by execution of the mate who had committed adultery (Deuteronomy 22:22); the other way was by a bill of divorce (Deuteronomy 24:1).

But when could the bill of divorcement be given, and what was its purpose? A man could give his wife a bill of divorce when he found "some indecency" in her. Such wording raised arguments? What is indecent? Some said *only* adultery. That didn't fit, because God had already outlined what to do when adultery was the issue. Others said that "indecency" referred to anything the husband didn't like, such as wearing the hair over the shoulders, talking too loudly, speaking with men in public, etc. In fact, these were popular reasons for divorce when Jesus was alive.

However, that was far too liberal an interpretation of "indecency." The Hebrew word for indecency means "nakedness." Indecency in Deuteronomy 24:1 probably referred to sexual perversion.

Notice that God did not command the divorce. He *did* command that a bill of divorce be given to the wife. He did this because the hearts of the husbands were so hard that they would kick the wives out without freeing them to marry someone else. That meant that the wives had to resort to begging or prostitution.

The bill of divorce allowed the woman to marry someone else. In fact, it was really a declaration of independence or a bill of freedom.

It is clear that the divorce freed the parties to marry someone else. God recognized the new marriage as legitimate. He did not say that a new marriage constituted a continuous state of adultery. In fact, he called the divorced woman who remarried "another man's wife" and spoke of her second husband as her "latter husband" and her first husband as "her former husband" (Deuteronomy 24:2-4).

It is true that God hated divorce in the Old Testament (Malachi 2:14, 16). But that does not mean that He did not forgive divorce.

Jesus and Divorce

By the time Jesus entered His ministry, divorce and remarriage had become the popular thing to do. Many adults in Jesus day had been divorced and remarried several times. The historian Seneca records that people got married in order to get divorced and got divorced in order to marry again.

Jesus stressed God's original intention for marriage (Matthew 19:3-8; Mark 10:2-12; Luke 16:18). He also taught that divorce could dissolve a marriage. Read Matthew 5:31, 32; 19:9.

160

Because the "except" clause does not appear in Mark 10:11, 12 and Luke 16:18, does not mean we should delete it from Matthew 5:31, 32 and 19:9. To hear Jesus' whole teaching on any subject requires listening to all that He says on the subject. His teachings in the four Gospels are not in competition with each other. What He says in one place does not cancel out what He says in another place. His teachings in different places and on different occasions supplement one another.

When immorality was the reason for the divorce, then a man did not commit adultery by marrying another person nor did he cause his divorced wife to commit adultery if she married another. But what is meant by "immorality"? The Greek word for immorality is *porneia*. It is used twenty-six times in the New Testament, and it refers to any kind of sexual perversion. It cannot be restricted to any one sexual category such as extramarital sex or premarital sex. It can include homosexuality, lesbianism, exhibitionism, beastiality, incest, etc.

Jesus did not demand divorce in such cases, but He allowed it. The ideal is for repentance, forgiveness, and reconciliation to follow sexual sin. But when such situations do lead to a divorce, then remarriage is possible. The word for divorce means a total release. The divorce is the granting of freedom to marry someone else.

Paul and Divorce

Paul emphasized God's original intention (Romans 7:2, 3; 1 Corinthians 7:10, 11, 39), but also taught that divorce could dissolve a marriage if that's what an un-Christian partner wanted (1 Corinthians 7:12-16, 27-28). To say, "The brother or the sister is not under bondage in such cases . . ." (1 Corinthians 7:15) means that the person is free to marry another.

"Un-Biblical" Divorces

One problem facing us today is this: What should we do about people who are divorced for reasons other than those allowed in the Bible, and then marry someone else?

Jesus did not address himself directly to this problem. His teaching was designed to curb the wholesale divorce for any cause that was so common in His day. Many of His audience would have been divorced and remarried. Jesus did not condemn them in their present state, nor did He tell them that they were living in a continual state of adultery. Neither did He tell them to return to their

161

first mates. The situation of meeting the woman at the well (John 4) gave Jesus the ideal opportunity to say all of the above thoughts, but He didn't.

When the woman told Jesus she had no husband, Jesus replied, "You have well said, 'I have no husband'; for you have had five husbands: and the one whom you now have is not your husband" (4:17, 18). Jesus did not say, "You have had one husband and have been living in adultery ever since." He did not even say, "Wrong. You do have a husband, your first. You are still married to him. Go back to him." Jesus evidently recognized her previous divorces and remarriages, but He did not recognize her living with a man as being in a marital state.

It is possible that she had been widowed five times; but in light of the popular custom of divorce and remarriage, that does not seem likely. It is also possible that she had been divorced five times for the right reason (sexual immorality on the part of her husbands), but that is doubtful; men did most of the divorcing, not the women. I believe she had been divorced and remarried five times; each man was called her husband except for the one with whom she was presently living.

Why didn't Jesus condemn her for her divorce? Wasn't she living in adultery ever since that first divorce? I doubt it. The New Testament does not clearly state that a person is *continuously* living in a state of adultery after an illegitimate divorce. It is possible that only the *initial* act of remarrying constitutes adultery. It is possible that the initial act of adultery committed by remarrying severs the covenant relationship; then the new union is considered a marriage. Although it began in an adulterous encounter, it need not remain so. Jesus never said that remarried people were living in continuous sin: that has been the conclusion of men. If remarriage constituted continuous adultery, I suspect He would have clearly stated it. Living in continuous state of adultery would be living in continuous unrepented sinfulness. The children would be technically illegitimate, and the church would have a case for exercising the kind of discipline applied in 1 Corinthians 5. But whichever way you understand the adulterous situation, we must not forget that God is a forgiving God.

God has never made it a practice to accept only those people who have made perfect decisions in the past. Jesus did not condemn that woman at the well or tell her to return to her first husband, but this does not mean He was approving of her actions.

Neither was He locking her up into her past. Instead, He was giving her hope for her future and demonstrating for us what God does in such situations (John 1:18). Her future indeed became much brighter, and she led a city-wide revival.

It is hard for many people to accept the grace of God with relation to divorce and remarriage. Many will think that I am saying that God approves divorce and remarriage. Many will think, "Well, if God is like that, then anyone can get a divorce and remarry—God will forgive."

The mature Christian does not seek loopholes to take advantage of God's grace. The Christian understands unrighteousness hurts God. He also understands that God's kindness toward us is not designed to encourage us to repeat our sins, but rather to lead us to repentance (Romans 2:4). Of course, some may take advantage of God's forgiveness, but that will not cancel God's grace. We must not deny God's grace to all just because some misuse it.

Divorce and remarriage is not what God wants in His creation, nor what we want in our country. But let's face it. Divorce and remarriage are what we have! We must teach in such a way as to slow down the trend; yet we need to minister to those many people who are hurting because of the pain of divorce and to those who feel they may be lost because of it. Let's reach out to both with God's truth and God's grace.

The Church and Divorce

The "locked-in" attitude. In this approach the church treats those who were unscripturally divorced and remarried as if they were eternally locked into their past failures. It is the belief that unless they abandon their present marriages, they are lost. They are living in a continual state of sin. Their children in the second marriage are technically considered illegitimate. A minister who uses this approach will refuse to counsel with anyone thinking about remarrying after a divorce; and, of course, he will not marry them.

To implement this approach consistently, the couples in question should be disassociated from the church. However, not many churches do that officially. Instead they do it personally—by looking down on the couple and their family, by shying away from them, and by not allowing them to get involved in the work of the church. As far as the church is concerned, they no longer have abilities that can be used for the Lord; they will no longer make any contribution to the family of God. They are not allowed to teach, to work with the youth, to help with the music program, or to do benevolent work. If they want to use their abilities in unselfish avenues, they will have to go to the Red Cross, volunteer to the local hospital, or help with community projects outside the church. These people are looked upon as having committed the unpardonable sin as long as their first mates are alive. They would be forgiven sooner if they had murdered their first wife or husband instead of divorcing her or him.

The "as if it never happened" attitude. This approach ignores the situation. The "marrying parson" models this attitude—if you want to get married, just knock on his door! The church with this attitude would never have an all-night prayer meeting for a member about to go through a divorce. A divorce is thought of as "just one of those things." Any hurt that is involved is overlooked. Divorce is "winked at"; thus divorces multiply—sometimes among Christian leaders.

The "revelational and redemptive" attitude. With this approach, the church offers help and service. The church will continue to uphold God's intentions for marriage without allowing current situations to stifle the teaching of God's Word about the permanence of marriage.

At the same time, the church will also offer a redemptive service for those whose marriges have failed, showing them the true character of God by forgiving and loving them. "All the paths of the Lord are lovingkindness and truth" (Psalm 25:10; 40:10; 85:10; 89:14; Proverbs 3:3; 14:22; John 1:14). This latter approach is what I consider to be the most helpful and pleasing to God.

Our children grow up with many erroneous ideas about marriage. Here are a few of them: (1) Marriage will sove all my problems. (2) If I get married, I will never be lonely again. (3) By marriage I can escape my parents. (4) Marriage is like an eternal date. (5) I will change him/her after we are married. (6) In marriage, our differences won't cause trouble. (7) Marriage is a trap or prison. (8) Marriage takes all the fun out of life. (9) Marriage is simply a legal piece of paper.

The church and the home must unite to tell the truth about marriage to young people *before* they get married. We must do more to prepare people for marriage. We need to teach the function for marriage for the permanence that God intended for marriage. We need to teach the realities and the practicalities of the relationship and erase the fantasies.

164

The church can help by offering special clinics and retreats for engaged couples, and by teaching Biblical guidelines for marriage in the youth groups. The church can decide to take Paul seriously by having the older women teach the younger women about marriage (Titus 2:3-5).

The church can also offer classes exposing the futility of divorce. Divorce is often not helpful, but hopeless, which is one of the reasons God hates it. He knows us and wants only what is good for us. Divorce is not a cure-all. Divorce is not what it is cracked up to be. To think that divorce is going to produce instant bliss is wrong. It is about time people heard about the suffering and problems that inevitably accompany marriage breakups.

Divorce brings terrible trauma for both children and adults. The children feel cheated and forsaken. They feel guilty, wondering if they are to blame. They want to love both parents, but they feel as if they are in a tug-of-war. The happiness of the holidays is marred by trying to decide which parent to be with.

Statistics show that second marriages are not any happier than first marriages, and have an even shorter life span. Aspirin cannot cure a brain tumor, and divorce cannot cure marriage problems; it only covers them up for awhile.

Before a couple remarries, the church needs to spend many hours teaching them about the ingredients of a successful marriage. If a person enters a second with the same erroneous ideas and habits he had in the first, another failure looms ahead. Don't think it could not happen again. Ninety percent of those who have experienced one divorce experience two.

The church is partly to blame. If divorced persons are made to feel like unforgiven sinners, then why should they hesitate to get a second divorce? Hell won't be any hotter with two divorces on the record. The church must actively seek to help make the second marriage a success.

Let's face it. Seldom is one mate *totally* innocent when a marriage is dissolved. Both people have contributed to the breakdown. Unless a person knows where he (or she) was wrong, admits it, repents of it, and changes, he will carry the weakness into the new marriage. Destructive interpersonal relationships will not hold a second marriage together anymore than they did the first one.

Too many people get married for the romance of it and the desire for personal happiness. Both of those reasons are self-oriented. Then when one mate (or both) does not get his way, he

165

thinks about severing the relationship. A marriage should be the result of the commitment of two people to one another, not to self. The love in a marriage should be the love expressed in 1 Corinthians 13:4-7. It is imperative that we tell the truth about both marriage and divorce.

We are all failures in certain areas of our lives. I doubt if any of us claim we have reached perfection. We have been cleansed from sin, but we still live with it. With this in mind, Christians must have open hearts and minds and reach out in love to those who are hurting because of divorce. Having love *(agape)* means to unselfishly meet another's needs; those who have been touched by divorce have many needs and must face many difficulties.

Look to the Future

Jesus opened the door toward a new future for the woman at the well (John 4). He did not ignore her past, but neither did He allow it to determine her future. A person who ignores his past failures or is drowning in guilt will not look to the future with any hope or security. The church can help people admit their errors, accept responsibility for their mistakes, and repent of them. Only then can a person be open to the forgiveness of God. And only then can he live in a new marriage with a bright future ahead.

I do not mean by this that we should never use the divorced leader in the work of the church. It would depend on the attitudes shown and on the individual situation. We must not conclude that divorce automatically calls for discipline. The reasons behind the divorce are important. We also must not conclude that divorce never calls for discipline. But all discipline must be done with redemption in mind.

The Need to Feel Worthy

Divorce can make all those involved feel a sense of failure; personal self-esteem can lower a great deal. We in the church need to remember that a person's failure in one area of life does not mean he will fail in all areas. We need to go out of our way to make the divorced feel they are still worthy human beings.

I know of one woman who moved in with her parents (her father was a preacher) after her divorce. She was an expert in working with children, so the church put her in charge of the ministry to children. What a blessing she has been to that church! I have never seen anyone handle children any better. What a tragedy it would

166

have been if that church had felt "failure in one area means failure in all." The Bible does not teach that God takes away from a divorced Christian God's charisma or gifts of service. The *divorcee* still has abilities to dedicate to God.

But what about being an elder or deacon? Does the "husband of one wife" mean a divorcee is automatically and eternally disqualified? That is one possible interpretation. But I interpret the characteristics for qualifying a person as an elder or deacon as applying not to his past history, but to his present character. If we run "husband of one wife" through all his past, then we must do the same thing with all the other characteristics. That means if a man was quarrelsome or a drunkard or a lover of money twenty years ago he can't serve as elder or deacon today. To take that position is to deny what God can do in a person's life. The characteristics for an elder or deacon spotlight a man's present character. They do not review his past history.

The Need for Friendship

A divorced person experiences many changes in personal relationships—with the mate, with the children, with in-laws, with friends of the couple, with the church. Sometimes jobs or residences are changed. Often a homemaker has to find a job to make a living; many times she has never worked before outside the home.

God is concerned about those who have been seriously uprooted and feel forsaken. His church should express similar concern by gathering the divorced into a loving fellowship. Communication lines should be kept open. The divorced person should be invited into the homes of other Christians. The church should consider beginning a ministry to single adults, so they will feel a part of a group that eats together and has fun together. If a congregation is too small, it should join with other area congregations to effectively minister to needs.

The Needs of the Children

While children are growing, they need input from both sexes to establish their identity and to feel good about their lives. With over one million children living with only one parent, it is time the church started to be more aware. The children's classes should be taught by male/female teams. Men in the church should create opportunities to spend time with children who don't live with their father.

167

Likewise, Christian women should build relationships with mother-less children.

Children of couples who have been divorced and remarried should not be treated as second-rate by the church. The children are not to blame, so why should they be punished? There are many ways to punish children; the worst way is to attack their self-esteem by looking down on them or ignoring their needs.

Practical Problems

Besides all the emotional difficulties, divorced people face many practical problems. The woman may need help with handling business—budgeting, buying insurance, home repairs, auto repairs, buying a house and car, job hunting, or getting financial aid. A man may need to know about cooking, cleaning, laundry, or caring for children's sickness.

The church can help see that these needs are met. I suggest that there be a special committee whose job it is to look into these matters and see what the needs are in each situation. We cannot assume that these matters will be taken care of by "somebody."

A divorced person should not expect all the initiative and effort to come from others. Here are some suggestions:

Do not bury your abilities. If your congregation is determined not to use your abilities, then find a church that will. Get involved. You don't have to be the "big cheese" or have the approval of the elders to give yourself away in service. Find someone who needs your help and give it. Anyone in the hospital? Anyone shut in at home? Anyone need a baby-sitter? Anyone need a good hot meal? Anyone need someone to shop for him? Anyone need to "get away" from the pressures of life by going to a concert or a play?

Don't remain in a rut. Develop your interests. Take a class. Join a club. Take a trip. Read a new book. Start a Bible club in your home for the neighborhood children. Visit the local nursing home. Redecorate your home and do all the work yourself. Get busy. Don't sit around feeling sorry for yourself.

Keep up your physical appearance. Even though you think no one cares how you look, visit the beauty shop or barber-shop regularly. Why not try a new haristyle or a different set of frames for your glasses?

Be mindful of your attitude. Don't fret about what other people think or let their reactions control your actions. Forgive your former mate. Don't be bitter or critical. Admit your faults, repent, and change. Accept God's forgiveness. Trust in God's love completely.

Keep morally pure. It might be easy to use the divorce as an excuse to fail in other areas of life. Don't turn to drink, illicit sex, gambling, or cheap thrills to bury your guilt or bitterness. Remember you are God's child! You can use this experience to mature into the likeness of Christ. Jesus has both glory and grace to share with you.

Don't jump into another marriage. If you can't see what you contributed to the divorce and have not changed, don't marry anyone—yet.

For Consideration or Discussion

Agree or Disagree:

1. Divorce is always a sin. Agree_____ Disagree_____ Discuss it.
2. When divorce occurs, two people are always at fault. Agree_____ Disagree_____ Discuss it.
3. When divorce occurs, the responsibility may be shared partly by the couple, by society, by parents, and by the church. Agree_____ Disagree_____ Discuss it.
4. The church can do something to reduce the divorce rate. Agree_____ Disagree_____ If you agree, discuss what the church can do.
5. The church should treat divorced persons no differently than other persons. Agree_____ Disagree_____ Discuss it.
6. Divorced persons may be elected as elders or deacons. Agree_____ Disagree_____ Discuss it.
7. The church could be more helpful to divorcing or divorced persons. Agree_____ Disagree_____ If you agree, discuss ways the church might help these persons.
8. *Addendum:* If you have been divorced, and if you are willing to share that with the class, talk about:
   a. How it feels to be divorced.
   b. How I would like the church to respond to me, a divorced person.
   c. What I, a divorced person, would like to say to someone contemplating divorce.

The Problem
Clinic

19

Marriage is not all problems, but problems will arise even in the best of marriages. Most problems between married partners can be resolved happily by Christlike persons who have proper interpersonal communication.

Marriage does not necessarily make a person different. Husbands often say, "My wife has made me grouchy." Such a statement is doubtful. Family living has a remarkable way of bringing out a person's real characteristics. The real person is revealed. When problems arise, it is important not to look for the faults in the mate. Instead, look for weak spots within oneself. Fill in the weak spots with the unselfish act of giving self for the other's good. Let your reactions spring from your inner self, not from the actions of another. If you react to a person in the same manner he acts toward you, you are not being controlled by the indwelling Christ.

James speaks explicitly on this point. He wrote that each Christian will encounter all kinds of trials that will test his character (James 1:2). These trials are for the purpose of testing his faith. When the trials come, he should display endurance in having God's kind of reaction to them (vv. 3, 4). To do this, each Christian needs wisdom, which James tells us God is willing to provide (v. 5). This does not refer to intellectualism, but to the characteristics James describes (3:13ff): "Who among you is wise and understanding? Let him show by his good behavior his deeds in the gentleness of wisdom." This wisdom from God is "first pure [without ulterior motives], then peaceable, gentle, and easy to be entreated [open to reason], full of mercy and good fruits, without partiality, and without hypocrisy [insincerity]" (v. 17).

Situations should not determine our lives. The characteristics we pour into those situations should be the determining factors. The solution to many marital problems can be discovered, if the two people involved list the situation in a middle column, like Christlike characteristics on one side, and opposite characteristics on the other. Then each mate should examine himself to see which of the two opposing attitudes he is pouring into the threatening situation. Some of these attitudes and their opposites are: peaceable/striving, gentle/harsh, reasonable/stubborn, kind/unkind, self-controlled/tempermental, jealous/not jealous, humble/arrogant, forgiving/resentful, thoughtful/inconsiderate, gracious/ungracious, honest/dishonest.

While one mate may be strong in his action, the other should not be wrong in reacting. Consistent expression of Christ's way by one person can revolutionize the relationship of a family.

Let us consider some specific problems and possible solutions:

1. *Who should manage the finances?* The one who is more responsible and capable in keeping records straight. If the wife handles the money, she must remember that this is a delegated responsibility; and she must manage the budget in keeping with the life goals of the household.

2. *Should both the husband and wife work?* This is becoming a common practice. Families have varying situations, so it is impossible to make a general rule for all persons to follow. Both persons, however, should ask themselves why they are both working. Is it to meet the necessities of the family, or just to keep up with the crowd? Once the wife's salary is budgeted to help with the monthly bills, there is no easy exit in sight. If her salary could be used for extras only, she could later discontinue working without undue hardship.

3. *My husband wants sex too much.* What can I do about it? Read 1 Corinthians 7:1-7. Your husband has been planning on sex with you even before the wedding. He fully expects sex after the wedding, even though you may not have had any indication that he was so "sex-minded." Your relationship has changed now that you are married, and you have a responsibility in that change. Be thankful that he loves you. He could have his sex needs met elsewhere, if you do not seek to fulfill them.

4. *We do not want to have children.* Is this wrong? Many young couples feel this way. Other people must not cause them to feel unacceptable if they are childless. Sexual expression is not just for

171

creation of life, but also for the cementing of love. Although in the Bible children are considered to be a blessing (Psalm 127:4, 5), there is no "thus saith the Lord" that a couple should have children to be happy. Neither does the Bible inform us as to when a couple should have children or how many. Furthermore, birth control is not Biblically wrong; however, living just for oneself is wrong. Each couple should examine their motives.

5. *My husband does not show me physical affection except in bed.* What can I do? How do you look when he comes home from work? Look nice, smell nice, smile, and grab him! Show him physical affection, and it will be returned.

6. *My wife is fat and sloppy and unattractive.* Why? Is she working all day without modern conveniences? Do you give her a reason to look nice by taking her out to eat or to a movie? Do you buy her pretty clothes and compliment her when she does look nice? Compliment her on her looks, especially in public. Sweet talk her like you did when you were courting!

7. *Who is responsible for the children's discipline when the father is gone?* Specifically, the mother is; however, the matter of child discipline should be discussed and agreed upon before the situation arises. If this is done, one parent will uphold the other when both are involved. When one parent is absent, the other will administer discipline in agreement with the other parent. To delay discipline until the father comes home is not effective discipline. Furthermore, the children will dread to see their father come home.

8. *What should be done if in-laws continually interfere?* A couple can permit the in-laws to volunteer advice. Listening to them we meet a need of theirs. Listen without comment, and then do what the two of you have agreed upon. Never allow in-laws to polarize you. If they become insistent or overbearing, be honest enough to tell them how you feel. Explain that you are a new family unit over which the husband is the head.

9. *What should parents do when their unwed daughter gets pregnant, or their son is the one involved?* Do not add a wrong reaction to a wrong action. Do not force the two to marry, if a lifelong commitment is obviously not desired. Do not act just to "save face." The only difference between this sin and the sins you commit is that theirs becomes obvious. Whether or not the daughter should keep the child will depend upon the unified decision of the family, after considering the welfare of both the child and the mother.

172

10. *What would you advise for a family in which the husband and wife are of different faiths?* This need not be the tragedy that some people make it. Of course, nagging or belittling the other's position is never wise. God wants the man and wife to live in peace. Providing that both have centered their "faith" in Jesus Christ, the following approach may help:

List the areas of agreement between the two religions. You may be surprised to find that you agree far more than you disagree. Thank God together for the specific points of agreement. Read and discuss the Bible together, systematically and regularly. Study openly together the areas of disagreement, but do not allow the study to blur the points of agreement. Let the points of disagreement be seen in the Scriptural context, with the aim to understand truth and not to support a personal position. Decide together to let the Bible be the authority. The study should consider all the Bible says about a certain question. Do not argue about your differences. Ask, "Is this difference essential to Christianity?" Practice the patience and loving-kindness of God.

11. *What if the husband has interests and activities that are uninteresting to the wife, or vice versa?* The one should try to learn about the other's interest. Read about it, ask questions, join in it, and try to develop an interest. If that is not possible, allow the other to pursue the activity without complaining or sarcasm. Develop your own interest or hobby that you can pursue when he/she is occupied. In other words, respect the desires and keep busy yourself. Plan and encourage activities that you both enjoy, and spend some time together. Make these times so pleasant that the mate will want to have more of these "together" times than "apart" times.

12. *How can we foster family togetherness?* Do things together around the house. Make it a family project to wash the car, plant shrubbery, paint the house, or rearrange the furniture. Have home parties with popcorn, cokes, and sandwiches, or have an indoor picnic on the floor. Let the whole family contribute in making a pizza, adding the ingredients each likes best. Sing together, play together, sit around a campfire in your own backyard, or sit on the patio and listen to the sounds of nature. Play outdoor games. Turn off the TV and communicate with each other. Play board games that involve the whole family. Ask the children for their opinions and advice about family plans and purchases. Let the whole family take part in buying a house or car. Take the children with you when you buy a present for your mate. Include the children in conversa-

tions about work, finances, or decisions. This will help them to understand and accept the fact that they cannot have everything they want. Plan your vacations together: the schedule, route, activities, places to stay. Read the Bible together. Choose a passage that applies to a specific need or problem in the family. Allow each family member to raise questions. Discuss together the implications of the Scripture. Pray together for specific needs by naming friends of all the members.

13. *How can I keep my wife feeling that she is a person with dignity?* Recognize her charisma (gift), and encourage her to use it. Praise her abilities in front of others. Pass on to her the compliments you hear about her. Trust her. Don't make jokes about her to others. Do not criticize, belittle, or oppose her in front of the children. Protect her against their rebellion. Do not allow them to show disrespect or disobedience. Support her disciplinary measures. Help her once in a while with the housework. Occasionally stay at home with the children so she can go out by herself or with a friend. Take her with you to as many public gatherings as you can. Tell her you love her. Share with her your dreams and desires. Take time to satisfy her in the sex act.

14. *What should be done when a husband spends much of his time at the office or traveling in his work?* If the husband's absence from home is because his job necessitates it, and he is happy in that work, it is up to the wife to accept the unalterable circumstances and adjust to them. It is much better to have a husband who is happy and contented, even though absent, then to have a husband who is restless and unhappy, even though at home. If the wife is lonely and bored while he is away, she can become involved in service for others, hobbies, and keep in contact with friends and neighbors. When her husband comes home, she should devote herself fully to him, keeping the household tasks to a minimum, preparing his favorite foods, and listening to his adventures. Make his time at home a time of great quality, since it cannot be of great quantity. When the husband comes home from a trip, he should devote time to the family. He shouldn't plunge immediately into his business at home. Also, if he has been away very long, his wife has been making all the decisions. She will need time to adjust to the fact that the head of the family is back.

If the absence is voluntary and not necessary, the wife should then examine herself and the home atmosphere. Is she bitter, angry, and upset whenever he is home? Are all of her duties and

174

services burdensome? Is the house cluttered? Is he a person who likes everything in its place? Is it such a showplace that he is not free to remove his shoes while he reads the newspaper? Perhaps the wife is not in agreement with his type of work and pleads with him to change. Maybe she is so independent and self-sufficient that she does not seem to need his presence at all. If any of these hit the target, the two need to work at being one in their life goals.

The Church's Responsibility to Families

This entire book has called for an emphasis on family togetherness. Our complex multischeduled lives prevent the family from being together, unless we get our priorities in place. Let us not be an activity-controlled people. The church should not be a factor in keeping family members apart all week. Here are some suggestions for churches:

1. *Develop the philosophy that the church exists for families, not vice versa.* Evaluate every lesson, every sermon, and every activity according to how it will affect the family life of the members.

2. *Plan activities that the family can attend together.* Why have the youth program just for youth? What about having family programs? Why not rent the roller rink for the whole family once in a while? Let two or three families plan and present the evening worship program one Sunday a month.

3. *Recognize family units more.* The whole family could come forward when a member makes a decision for Christ. Have family members baptize one another.

4. *Use family units to serve Communion and take up the offering during worship service.* What Scripture restricts these tasks to elders and deacons? None!

5. *For one quarter of the year, the Sunday school could have a class for families.* Why split up the families every Sunday for years and years?

6. *Establish a Christian counseling center in the area.* Area churches could hire a Christian counselor who would be available for family counseling.

7. *Let your preacher be a family man.* Do not expect him to attend every meeting of the church. He needs some time at home with his family.

8. *Seek to utilize the members of the church* in combination with their family members, not in isolation from them.

9. *Each week publish in the church paper information about one*

175

family. Share their names, addresses, activities in school and community, careers, and church work.

10. *Finish all committee meetings on one or two nights a week,* instead of separting family members every night of the week.

The church must declare war upon the present trend to keep the family separated. Heaven will be God's family living together in unity. Let a foretaste of that reality be present here on earth. May each of us allow Heaven on earth as we let the image of God shine out of our hearts at home. If we have received the Holy Spirit, let us walk with Him and create and maintain the community of unity.

For Consideration or Discussion

Rate yourself:
Put a mark close to the characteristics which best describes you.

Peaceable . . . . Striving
Gentle . . . . Harsh
Reasonable . . . . Stubborn
Kind . . . . Unkind
Self-controlled . . . . Tempermental
Trusting . . . . Jealous
Humble . . . . Arrogant
Forgiving . . . . Resentful
Thoughtful . . . . Inconsiderate
Gracious . . . . Ungracious
Honest . . . . Dishonest

(If you have all the marks on the left side, you failed "humble!")

1. Discuss answers to the problems discussed in this chapter, and discuss any answer with which you disagree.
2. Discuss suggestions for developing a family oriented church.
3. Discuss how your church is measuring up to these suggestions.
4. Discuss whether your class can take the lead in implementing at least one of these suggestions.